MANAGEMENT SAVVY

How to Get It, How to Use It and
How to Become a Sparkling Leader

ROBERT E. LEVINSON

Trafford rev. 08/21/2014

 www.trafford.com
North America & international
toll-free: 1 888 232 4444 (USA & Canada)
fax: 812 355 4082

To my dad and my sons, Jon and Jim

My dad graduated from the University of Michigan in 1910 as an engineer. He soon became a sales engineer and sold all types of building materials. I was always inspired by his skill in working with people and ability to instill in them faith in his knowledge and sincerity. He had a knack of working well with employees and guiding them to be successful—which I hope will be passed on to you through the pages of this book. I dedicate this book to my dad and to my two sons, Jon and Jim, also successful businessmen, in gratitude and love.

INTRODUCTION

My business career began when I was only 7 years old with a lemonade stand. My mother provided me with all of the supplies, and after I sold everything and showed my mother the cash, she proceeded to take out the cost of the supplies. I was left with very little when my mother told me, "You will have to learn how to figure the selling price after taking into consideration the costs."

Over the years, I was fortunate to be a part of a family business with my father and brother. As an owner and manager, I had the luxury of trying out various management ideas and techniques. This book is a collection of those ideas and techniques. In all of my writings, I have tried to provide ideas and methods to help you become a sharp and exciting manager, in addition to making you more successful.

After the sale of our family-owned business to American Standard, Inc., I accepted the position of Group Vice President for them in charge of 12 operating units and 3,000 people. When I left American Standard at age 65, I joined Lynn University in Boca Raton, Florida, as a Senior Development Officer. As of this writing, I am still employed at age 89.

I hope you enjoy this book and acquire some savvy management techniques that you can start using today.

Bob Levinson
2014

CONTENTS

ARE YOU HAVING FUN YET?

The surest way to get a little fun out of your business life is to help people grow to their fullest potential.

There's a company I know—a fun-less, sunless outfit. This company doesn't grow; it just stands still. Year after year, the company shows a moderate profit and the stockholders are apparently satisfied. It never occurs to them that with a little excitement and imagination the profits could be doubled. Still, profits or not, stockholder or not, the company is ailing. Why?

Because the people who work there are bored—stifled, frustrated, unhappy. And that goes for almost every employee from the president down. The point is this: It's not enough merely to exist. You have to grow. And, your people have to grow; they're entitled to. After all, their investment is bigger than any stockholder's. They're investing their lives!

What about your own skills and talent development? Are they sharply honed? Get a pad and pencil and write down the name of each person reporting directly to you, one name to a sheet.

Four questions to ask

Now ask yourself these four questions about each person and take the trouble to *write out* your answers under each name:

1. Are your department's goals and sub-goals crystal clear to this individual? Even more important, is *their* part in these various clear to them?
2. Are they motivated by an intense personal interest to help achieve these common goals?
3. Do you know exactly what skills they need to accomplish the job—and do they know?
4. Have you recently given them a new, challenging task with an unknown factor tied to it to excite their interest and exploit their unsuspected talents?

Solid, honest "yes" answers earn you five points per question. If you scored 20 for most of the people you supervise, you can come to work for me any time.

How to improve

How can you increase your score? Mainly by effort. A good manager should spend anywhere from 60 - 80% of his time training his people, both formally and informally, but always with a definite purpose in mind. This can include shop discussions, training by example and even a good employee-to-manager chat.

Training also includes special action programs, like one I used at Steelcraft. We called it "Mr. Steelcraft," and it's a way of giving out an ego booster shot.

Make them king for a day

One day I called an up-and-coming engineer named Jerry and asked, "Are you and Marge free tomorrow night?" They were. I told him an important distributor was coming to town for our training program and Jerry and Marge would be co-hosting him and his wife.

I wanted Jerry and Marge to take them out on the town and show them a good time with the company picking up the tab, of course. They were to entertain the company's important visitors that night.

Was Jerry delighted and flattered? Well, put yourself in his place. Most of your working life you're just another engineer. But for this one night, you are—unexpectedly—Mr. Big. You're personally delegated to charm a key company contact. And you're stepping out on the town, in the style of an executive earning three times your salary.

You win in five ways

For that one glorious night, Jerry was Mr. Steelcraft. It built his confidence and poise, helped him appreciate the problems of our distributors and gave the distributor, in turn, an insight into our manufacturing problems. It also made Marge an avid company fan and gave both of them a new incentive for achievement and success.

Try this in your own way. Make one of your people *your* Mr. Big for a day. Watch them burst with pride, glow with confidence. Watch them rally to your cause with the fervor of a loyal patriot. Now, *that's* fun! And it's profitable.

2

WANTED: MIRACLE MANAGERS FOR PLANT EMERGENCIES

On October 29, 1962, Cuba was blockaded. Our reserves were being called up. President John F. Kennedy was on the hot line to Moscow while at the same time attempting to calm the nation. Hundreds of emergency government calls must have gone out that day. One was a call I received in Cincinnati from the U.S. Army Engineer Procurement Office saying that special parts for bridge construction were desperately needed.

We had done this kind of work years back, but hadn't bid on a government contract in more than four years. Yet, my caller said he knew of no other supplier who could do the job in the allotted time. It was a matter of national emergency.

Six days to do the job

The job involved making 1,960 pieces for 32 different products weighing a total of some 80,000 lbs. We had no special tools, dyes or previous experience with these items and neither did our subcontractors—and the Army needed delivery in exactly six days.

Our top executive team discussed the matter and we agreed that we couldn't do the job in the allotted time any more than any other supplier could, but we had to. The entire contract would be put on a "hand-made" basis. Managers, supervisors, production and office people pitched in—and they were superb. Some few said the task was hopeless. They were ignored by the rest of the team.

The way to a miracle

We used what I call "the simultaneous equation," which simply means that all wheels turned at once. For instance, materials, parts and tools were being obtained before the contracts had been completely drawn up. You can do it if you have to. We also used "on-hand fueling," which typically meant that one of our executives would fly to a subcontractor's plant and stay there until that portion of the job was ready.

Not to drag out the story, we made delivery 12 hours ahead of time. Looking back, I can see that there were five factors involved—five elements that can help you organize your own miracle whenever a real emergency arises:

1. A general sense of urgency generated by top management
2. A refusal to take "no" from employees or subcontractors
3. The simultaneous equation
4. Use of on-hand fueling
5. No giving in to "hold-up people"

Hold-up people? Yes, they're the naysayers, the project blockers, the delayers. More than any other factor, the hold-up person can keep you from your goal. Over the years, I've made a list of common types:

- The detouring delayer. They write letters instead of getting on the telephone. Whatever is the longest route, that's the one they choose.
- The 'manana'-minded idler. Tomorrow is good enough for them. They never seize the day.
- The closed-minded resister. An open mind spots a shortcut. This person, however, resists any change in procedure or policy.
- The time-killer work slougher. They spend most of the day showing you why something can't be done—instead of trying to do it.
- The indecisive road-blocker. One of the worst. They can't make up their mind and would no more stick their neck out than fly to the moon.
- The lazy goal-defeater. They won't make an extra effort, such as cracking a book, putting in extra time or doing a new task.

Managers must work magic

As I look over the list, their names begin to sound like a strange species of birds. The indecisive road-blocker ... closed-minded resister ... can't you just see these feathered friends flapping around your project, setting up a noisy chatter?

But I am mixing my metaphors. Let's just say that whether they're "hold-up people" or "birds," you've got to win them over, correct their behavior—or gun them down.

In industry today, miracles are needed rather often and a leading company must be prepared to perform them. So must a leading government or union or trade association. So must the world itself, for that matter. And miracles are made by managers.

3

JOB VARIETY ADDS SPICE TO A WORKING MAN'S LIFE

If it comes to a choice between butterflies in the stomach and boredom—as it often does—I'll take the butterflies. So, I think, will most people. That's why I recommend "job variety" as a way to boost employee morale and production in just about any industry.

For years our company has kept its employees, or a large percentage of them, in a constant state of happy agitation. A draftsman never knows when he may be given a quick briefing and sent on a sales call. A data entry clerk may fill in as transportation clerk. An engineer is sent to troubleshoot. This keeps people alert and makes them grow.

A leader emerges

The young welder, for instance, whom we took off production and named instructor for a three-day distribution training session, turned out to be a real leader. Eventually, that welder was promoted to lead, then foreman and, ultimately, a traveling technician, solving distributor problems at every stop.

Said Schopenhauer: "The more we look forward to anything, the less we enjoy it when it comes."

We agree, so we never give any warning about these sudden temporary assignments in job variety. To tell the truth, of course, not everyone will look forward to them with pleasure. It's natural to be a little petrified at the idea of stepping outside your usual way of life on the job.

An introvert changes

One engineer, Dave, was a real talent, a veritable whiz in his field. But talk about introverts? I think he coined the word. He was a valued employee and I wanted him to grow, but it was essential to draw him out of his shell.

I'll never forget the day I called Dave into the office. "You've been elected," I told him bluntly.

He was wary. "Elected to what?"

"One of our executives has been requested to make a speech in Cleveland," I told him, "and you're clearly the best person for the job. Nobody else here knows the subject as well."

Quite clearly, his worry turned to panic. But I goaded him and shamed him into responding to the challenge. And now I can sum up his progress in four words—There's No Stopping Him.

A clerk gets a big order

John, on the other hand, asked for the chance. He had a routine job in the order department, but he was the one who took the call from a customer who was hopping mad. "That guy's really upset," he said. "I think the company should send somebody to him."

"Yes. When can you leave?"

He took off with apprehension and misgiving; he returned with a light in his eyes and a big fat order to wave before my eyes.

A worker gets out of a rut

Then there was Michael. He really had "the first time shakes." I called him out of the engineering department and told him that he had to go to Chicago to handle a troubled distributor. He just about refused. It was out of his sphere.

"Okay," I said. "You don't have to go. But you'll be sidestepping a worthwhile experience. You'll be admitting to yourself that you'll never broaden your experience, get out of your own little rut. You have an hour to decide."

Actually, he agreed in a few minutes. I briefed him on the distributor's complaint, told him to clarify certain procedures and give them more information about product use.

Two days later, he was back. Talk about windbags. Talk about excitement. I couldn't shut him up. He had fielded most of the questions well, had made notes where his knowledge was light. He filled in the gaps and got back to the distributor on the telephone.

They feel like the owner

He felt like a big operator, but more than that —he acted as if he owned the place. And that was the idea.

Any employee who acts like the owner will use his judgment and skill and exhibit values you would like. And he'll get ahead, too. Act like the owner. Not bad advice for you, in your own career.

4

DON'T LET YOUR INITIATIVE CONK OUT

What reason, more than any other, keeps people from advancing in their jobs? The inability to get along without the boss's help. The secret word is *initiative*.

There are these six common obstacles to initiative:

1. Lack of training
2. Failure to fully analyze
3. Lack of profit awareness
4. The waiting game
5. Fear of idea rejection
6. Believing the job is too tough

Ask yourself: Do I know enough about this subject to go ahead with it? No? Then I must read that book or register for that course—in short, do whatever is necessary to bolster my knowledge. This type of roadblock may be keeping me from moving ahead on projects that should— otherwise would be—getting my attention.

Analyze fully. Savvy managers squint into every nook and cranny, learning all they can about a problem. They work with the point person at the plant; sit down with the assistant at their desk. They never try to solve a problem without being fully acquainted with the facts. Failure to analyze means a bum start.

Never forget profit

Imagine a football game. Ten players are devoted to scoring a touchdown. The eleventh is interested in getting a batter out at home plate. Somebody screwy? You bet. Number 11 doesn't know the name of the game. And, in business, the name of the game is profits. A good manager never loses sight of this.

Waiting is a bad habit. Chances are that if it has become a habit, a manager has been remiss too. They have failed to stroke the fires of an employee's enthusiasm, destroyed their initiative.

Rejection fear is widespread and usually unfounded. Ideas are too urgently needed today. A good idea is usually good for everyone concerned. Even if the idea doesn't work, you'll be better off for taking the initiative.

Job too tough? Could be. Especially if you haven't taken the first steps to train yourself, to analyze. But once these steps have been taken, apprehension should end.

Ten ways to stay ahead

What this all boils down to is a lesson in staying ahead of your boss. Here is a ten-point program to get you started:

1. Firmly resolve to take off on your own more than you have. Go to the boss only when you've exhausted all other possibilities.
2. Be aggressive. Don't be pushy, but be constructively aggressive. You don't have to tread on another person's toes or usurp someone's

authority. But, most bosses welcome an employee's initiative.

3. Build on the foundation of a good idea. Inject new enthusiasm into it. Reinforce it with positive, profit-directed attitudes.

4. Motivate your people to self-starting profit performance. Keep them aware of the possibilities of attaining their objectives.

5. Develop self-starters. Some need a gentle push to get them going. Train 'em—inspire 'em—to act on their own.

6. Make a big deal out of every idea proposed. Help your people to convert small notions into large money-savers.

7. Practice dollar diplomacy. Track down savings. Don't wait for the boss. And train your people to respond in the same way.

8. Cash in on every moment of potentially productive time. A profitable idea may occur in the barber's chair, during a walk, while traveling to or from your work place.

9. Question. Analyze all operations you control. Savvy questions remain alive until answered.

10. Keep a weather eye out for roadblocks in your department. Always keep in mind the obstacles to initiative we have listed and apply them as a kind of test to each person who works for you.

Many self-starters have at one time been slow starters or non-starters. But, some savvy manager injected the fuel to keep the engine from conking out, to help power it into an independently operating unit.

5

BRAINSTORMING TECHNIQUES—HOW YOU CAN TAME YOUR WILD IDEAS

Brainstorming. Some people just don't believe in it. They contend that idea conception is a one-person job and group sessions are practically worthless.

I don't agree. I believe that thoughts are fissionable, that most good ideas result from the interaction of other ideas.

Out of brainstorming comes new approaches, new techniques. Its sessions can broaden your scope, expose you to the other fellow's point of view, often for a helpful change.

Encourages timid

Brainstorming sessions encourage the timid to speak up. They sharpen your abilities to express yourself, to persuade others to your point of view, to "think on your feet" and to extemporize.

The benefits of brainstorming are multiple. But many managers are skeptical, to say the least. A friend of mine recently said, with a hint of scorn in his voice, "You mean to tell me that you have time to sit in on meetings and listen to a lot of wild ideas?"

Precisely. Wouldn't miss it for the world. Not only that, it's profitable. And if for no other reason, brainstorming is a perfect way to get a better insight into your employees.

What's the matter with a wild idea anyway? Like the airplane? Or television? Or even sending a man to the moon? Give me a few wild ideas like those anytime.

Provides variety

There are a number of reasons why that, at our company, we used brainstorming session as a source of possible solutions and invention. For one thing, it got as many people as possible into the act, and thus provided variety in our decision-making processes.

We draw on the expertise of workers engaged in different activities in different areas of the company. There's nothing at all wrong with having the advertising manager sit in on a production meeting. Maybe their perspective will bring fresh approaches to problem-solving.

Simple techniques

Few managers know how to get the most out of brainstorming sessions. There are a couple of simple techniques that can help:

- Create the right climate. For brainstorming sessions to be fully effective, you must create the proper atmosphere for a perfectly free expression of idea and opinion. Give everyone at the session a chance to say whatever pops into their mind.
- Do not do anything to intimidate participants.

There should not be criticism simply for the sake of criticism. No one should be made to feel foolish about what they have said or that they might somehow be "penalized" for being "too far out." The idea is to get the ball rolling and keep it rolling. Inhibitions must be removed to the greatest possible extent.

Chain reactions, wild ideas

"Now here's the problem, what can we do about it?"

"Hey, great idea. What do you think, George?"

"Pretty good suggestion, but it might irritate some of our customers a bit. How about if we modified it some to..."

Chain reaction. One thought giving birth to another. The harvest you'll reap will be about 98% chaff and 2% wheat, but, believe me, that 2% is definitely worth every second of the time you spend in brainstorming. Sure. Why not? What would happen if you sent someone a triangular sales letter? They couldn't file it. So maybe they would just toss it away.

On the other hand, since it wouldn't file very easily, maybe they will read it—maybe just because it'd be so peculiar looking. And maybe, just maybe, because they couldn't do anything else with it, they would act on it. Worth a try?

Remember that friend of mine who doesn't like brainstorming sessions, let alone wild ideas? Maybe we could even change his mind. Maybe we could mail him a large triangular envelope...

6

LOOK AT THE PLUSSES OF NEW IDEAS— HOW YOU CAN ENCOURAGE SUGGESTIONS

Have you ever had someone dump cold water on one of your ideas? Of course you have. Everyone has. It can be an extremely deflating experience. You were all fired up with a really good idea to save your company money, to improve a product or to simplify a system.

In your enthusiasm, you presented your idea to someone—and he or she looked at you as though you were stupid. Then they said something like, "I've heard that before," or "I'm sure it won't work," or maybe, "That doesn't make sense."

Instead of watering your idea to make it bloom, they drowned it in cold water.

Discourages originator

But cold water can and frequently does more than just douse an original idea. It often discourages the originator from coming up with more suggestions later on. And one of them could be the best one your company has ever had.

How does the savvy manager handle someone with an idea? They listen attentively. Then they evaluate the idea, concentrating on its plusses, rather than its minuses. If the idea isn't so hot, they let the person who thought of it down gently.

Just how do you turn down someone's idea without turning them off as a source of future suggestions? I faced that problem once.

One of our employees at Steelcraft, let's call him George, came to me with an idea that sounded quite good at first. After I thought about it, though, I realized that it wasn't really possible.

George suggested that we set up a fund through automatic companywide payroll deductions to take care of the office solicitations that seem to plague every business. Every time someone has a birthday, gets married or has a baby, the hat is passed. These solicitations always disrupt work and often generate hard feelings.

Can cause more trouble

Now don't get me wrong; I think it's great that people care enough about fellow employees to give gifts. But I can't help feeling that the solicitation causes more trouble than it's worth. We'd been looking for a way to stop or control it for quite a while.

However, George's idea would probably generate more problems than it would solve for us. For example, it would add considerably to our bookkeeping load, and there'd also be the problem of how much to spend for each occasion. Of course, there would continue to be those persons who felt that gift giving didn't belong in the business world.

If I had told this to George, it would have deflated his ego—because I would have been dousing his idea right at the peak of his enthusiasm.

So I said, "Interesting idea. Contributions have been giving us concern. Let's think about it some more and discuss it tomorrow."

He left with a smile. The boss was considering his idea.

The next day, after his excitement had calmed down, we had a give-and-take session during which I gradually pointed out the flaws in his ideas. I was squelching the idea without squelching George.

"Show me" attitude

Savvy managers don't blindly accept every idea to come along just because it's new, of course. They encourage the "show me" attitude. They want their employees to be able to prove that the idea is good and can really work. This encourages them to use their imagination and initiative, to think the idea through.

But don't overdo it and create the image of yourself as a closed-minded guy. You can easily give the impression of being anti-everything. When that happens, it won't be long before you sap the enthusiasm of everyone you work with.

You can still go ahead and look for problems and flaws. By all means, search obstacles and objectives.

But if you cultivate the ability to concentrate on the strengths of an idea, you'll have one of the keys to business success. And many good ideas will constantly keep coming your way.

7

HOW TO GET AHEAD

Don't bother to read this if you're content to stay where you are, be it second-, third- or fourth-echelon management. This is addressed to the person who wants to grow—the one who's aiming for the personal, professional and financial rewards that come from becoming a top-level savvy manager.

The best way to make it to the top in any company is to become the person they run to when the going gets tough. Such a person is inevitably the most respected one in their company. Their name comes up in every conversation—including the ones about promotion.

How do you become your company's official resident expert on everything?

Well-planned campaign

A well-planned campaign that has years-ahead progress in mind. Since the prime ingredient in the campaign is you, the way to start is with some searching self-analysis. Step one: Define your present situation. You can't get anywhere without knowing where you are when you start. Here's how to go about getting up your "personal know-how" questionnaire.

On one sheet of paper answer the following questions candidly:

1. What profit-making ideas have you come up with in the last six months?
2. On what sort of matters do most people come to you for advice?
3. What do you enjoy most about your work?
4. What special skills do you have? List the unused ones as well as the used.

The answers to these questions should give you a pretty good idea of your strengths.

The hard part

Now—and this is the hard part—for a listing of your weaknesses.

On another sheet, answer these questions:

1. What kind of work takes you too long to do?
2. On what kind of assignments do you most often seek help because you lack the confidence to complete them on your own?
3. What kind of work do you consistently put off or try to avoid?
4. What additional responsibilities should you be tackling but aren't?

If you've answered both groups of questions honestly, you have a fair indication of how you stack up vis-à-vis your particular job. The trick is to identify your strong and weak points as they relate to your present job, the job you're currently shooting for, and, when that is achieved, the job after that. Knowing this information will help guide you in preparing, studying and qualifying as the resident expert.

And what about areas you're not directly involved with, but ones you work in from time to time? Since it's your aim to grow, the things you're occasionally involved with are natural avenues for you to follow up.

On another sheet, list the functions that indirectly involve you. One by one, evaluate your understanding of these jobs by answering the questions on your "strengths" and "weaknesses" sheets.

Now your work is really cut out for you. Rank your strengths and weaknesses. The ones that affect your advancement are the most important. Place them at the top of the respective lists.

Turns minuses to pluses

With regard to your shortcomings, it's your job to get as many items as you can off the "weaknesses" list and onto the "strengths" list, beginning with the most critical ones.

As for your strong points, you want to bolster them. You want your name to come up every time there's a discussion on something you're knowledgeable about.

Now that you know your strong and weak points, how do you go about working with them to further your career? Of course, the answer will vary with the person and the situation. But here are some suggestions you can try:

Ask your spouse or partner's opinion. Who knows you better? He or she may turn out to be your best critic. Consider taking a night school course. Read all you can about the subject. Talk over your concern on the subject with someone who knows it well. They will be able to help you put your knowledge into perspective.

The more effort you put into correcting your weaknesses, the faster you'll become a savvy manager on the way up.

8

PUTTING TROUBLE TO WORK WITH YOU

"**W**hat's wrong?" That's one of those questions that savvy managers ask of themselves at least once a week, if not more often. After all, it's a manager's job to manage, isn't it? And part of the definition of manage is handling problems or heading them off.

It's far better to ask "What's wrong?" with things in your department than to have the boss ask the same question.

Meet problems head on

There's another point to make here, too. Don't shy away from trouble. It's part of what you were hired to handle in the first place, isn't it?

Trouble is what keeps you in business and also what helps you grow. I can't help wondering about the person who always complains of their troubles. What do they want anyway? Everything exactly the same—day-in and day-out?

Wade right in

Anyone can run a trouble-free department. It's the savvy manager who wades right in and wrestles with problems. Every problem they handle adds to their experience, therefore helping to make them a better manager. And, someday, if they get to the head of his company, it will be because they developed the ability to meet problems head on.

Anticipate trouble

To handle problems, though, you have to know they're coming. Anticipating problems is an important factor in solving them before they get out of hand. And you'll never know they're coming if you spend all your time in an ivory tower—like your office. At Steelcraft, we insisted that our managers get into the plant as often as possible to find out what's going on in their departments. The problems that they found were usually small ones. That's because they were out there to catch them early, before they began to snowball.

Ask how things are

The successful managers I know get around to see the team under them at least a couple of times a week, and usually more often than that. As they make their rounds, they ask, "How are things?" That's not just an idle question intended to make friends. It's aimed at searching out problems while they are still bite-sized.

Though these managers delegate responsibility to the team under them like pros, they also make it their business to keep informed on what's currently happening in their departments.

One word of caution here. You have to be genuinely concerned about what's going on in your department.

Don't think that you can fake concern and get away with it for long. You can't. People will soon find out that you don't really want the answer to "How are things?" and soon about all you'll hear is "Fine." Then you'll be no further ahead than if you had stayed in your office.

Here's a management savvy tip that'll give you satisfaction every day: Find at least one thing in your department every day that's not being handled as you'd like it to be. Then take steps right away—that same day—to correct the situation. Besides giving yourself the satisfaction of solving a problem, you'll be adding to your store of experience and helping to make yourself a better, more savvy manager and valuable employee to your company, too.

Get a small notebook

One thing that I found absolutely essential as I was troubleshooting around the plant is a small notebook. I've found that it's a mistake to trust things to memory—and I've always prided myself on being able to remember even the smallest details. But just the sheer number of things that a manager must remember gets to be a problem.

So, I carried a "black book" with me at all times. In it I jotted down difficulties when and where I found them. If I couldn't take on the problem right away, then at least I knew I've made a note of it so I would be able to tackle it sometime in the near future. The 25 cents that I spent on each notebook ranks among my best investments.

9

HOW TO SQUEEZE 70 MINUTES OUT OF EVERY HOUR

The savvy manager leads a well-rounded life—and a life that is well-organized for proper use of time. With demands placed on the modern business-person, it is common to hear, "Where am I going to find time to do this?"

You have to use your time imaginatively and productively. Rarely do I work more than 9 or 10 hours a day. Yet some managers tell me they have to work 11, 12 or 13 hours just to keep up! I think if they had a sensible, savvy approach to making the clock work for them, they'd be able to do 12 hours of work in 8.

You must become a "clock-watcher" in the most positive sense of the world. You must take time for must-do functions only. There are five basic areas of time that savvy managers should concern themselves with and stick to each day:

Must-do functions

1. *Start by planning your day in advance.* You can do this before arriving at the office—while showering, dressing or commuting to work. The first thing

I do each morning is to circulate among my key people. This is the time they know they can catch me with problems and questions and it helps finalize my day's plans.

2. *Give "people development" your priority.* Usually the first thing I do when I arrive at the office is to circulate among the key people. This is when they can catch me with questions or special problems, so I can assimilate possible interruptions or difficulties before completing that mental outline of my day. And always give top priority to training and development, for it is the key to management savvy. This is one area you should definitely *not cut.*

3. *Move at least one improvement step forward each day.* The trick is not to let one day pass by without a change for the better. Each day I select a different target for improvement—it may be the budget, selling efforts, scrap waste, etc. When you think improvements, you think like an owner. And there's no better way to get the owner's attention.

4. *Give your operation a daily once-over.* Make time to let your people see you in action. Your people need your leadership. I made it my business to go through my operation at least once a day. A little kindness here, a question there. It gives people reassurance and makes you appear a human being.

5. *Retain taskmaster control over everyday essentials.* Each job involves basic requirements, so make sure that you take care of those essentials and that you allocate enough time for each of them.

Your goal as a savvy manager is to expand your activities to achieve more on a given day. Some managers can't see the forest for the trees. Others are unable to see the hours for the minutes. I'm talking about time leaks—the kind that defeat any expansion goal. Avoid these pitfalls by identifying these leaks and plug them up when they occur. Be on the lookout for these five time-waste signals:

Time-waste signals

1. *Complaints.* If there are too many complaints, don't just waste time answering them—find out why there are too many complaints. A little time here will save hours later.

2. *Tongue time twisters.* You can talk time to death, on the telephone, face-to-face or with visitors who overextend their stays. Everyone likes to hear themselves talk. If you keep in mind the fact that you must be concise, you'll be surprised at the time you save.

3. *Paperwork pile-ups.* Sometimes I think every manager should have a scale on their desk. When the paper pile-up goes over a pound, then they should start thinking of cutting down and delegating.

4. *Idle time.* If there are people doing nothing, you must be doing too much. Delegate responsibility and free yourself for more constructive tasks.

5. *Efficiency drain.* Keep your eye trained for results, because when they don't live up to expectations, there's an efficiency breakdown. If there's a breakdown, you investigate, discover, solve.

Keep these thoughts in mind and you'll see how easy it is to squeeze 70 minutes out of every hour.

HOW TO HANDLE EMPLOYEES WITH SAVVY

Whatever field you're in—business, politics, sports—if you're a manager, you succeed through your people. You can have the brightest ideas and best systems in the world, but if you cannot succeed in motivating your people and rallying them behind you, you'll never get anywhere.

Therefore, how do you succeed? The formula is easy. You have to start out by picking the right people. Next, identify and tap their abilities. Finally, build their abilities and channel them in a direction toward achieving goals.

As a leader, you should stimulate performance, excite interest, perpetuate high standards and keep friction and resentment to a minimum. In short, the leader should pass what Walter Lippmann refers to as "the final test of a leader." The leader "leaves behind him in other men the conviction and will to carry on."

Don't get lost

I sometimes have had job applicants come to me and say, "I'd like to work for a company where you don't get lost in the crowd."

If you're a big company manager, it's a dangerous pitfall to guard against. If you're a small company manager, your task may be simpler, but if you fail in your task, the reasons will be less understood by your employees.

The truly savvy manager in any company—large or small—always takes positive action to make sure that their people never feel lost.

Assuming you're a small company manager, one of the things you can do to keep your people happy is to show them what your company has to offer compared to the giant operation on the other side of town, such as having the opportunity to work closely with key decision-making people.

As a savvy manager, your prime objective is to expand your span of control, to multiply the number of profit actions you take in a given period of time. This means that you keep your fingers placed in more pies—but, because of the reliance and trust that you have in your people you need only keep the tips of your fingers in. You exercise control with a ten-minute check instead of a two-hour appraisal. You do this because of your faith in your people. But faith doesn't just happen; you have to develop your people.

After you develop them, how do you know how much faith you can place in each person? Well, simply write down the name of each person who works for you. Then, list each major job function they perform. Now, analyze the amount of time you spend on each job and resolve to cut that time in half—without lowering standards of performance.

Train your people

How? By training your people to perform independently of you—by increasing their capabilities and freeing yourself for the more important, larger responsibilities that the savvy manager never has quite enough time for.

And, in case you don't know it, directly or indirectly, savvy managers spend 75% of their time guiding or instructing people. This doesn't have to be formalized; osmosis—or teaching by example—is just as effective a tool and can be easily used in guiding or instructing your employees.

Training is a highly individualized process. Each trainee has their own way of learning. One person will respond to pressure, another to a well-presented challenge, a third to a carefully calculated vanity prod. The idea is to experiment. Vary your strategy until you find the one that works best.

11

PUT YOURSELF ON THE HIRING LINE

For people to work well together there must exist among them a built-in chemistry, an ability to "get along."

This is especially important when you are hiring a new person. As a manager, it is often your responsibility to judge whether this person or that person is the correct one for a position of importance.

To function efficiently as a smooth-running, profit-minded team, your people must establish an agreeable blend, achieving a common understanding and acceptance. I call this "chemical responsibility." As a savvy manager, you cannot do your compounding too carefully.

All it takes is a single wrong element to dilute and weaken the formula. The trick to selecting a new employee is to project yourself into the minds of your people. Ask yourself the following questions:

- How will our people respond to the new person?
- How will the ingredients of his or her character and personality blend with the existing mix of our department or organization?
- Will he or she be comfortable in their association with the staff?
- Will the associates respect them and will they respect the associates?

Select the right man

You will often be faced with the task of selecting candidates and interviewing them for important positions in your company. When we were faced with that problem—our Canadian division needed a manager—we devised a plan to assure the selection of the right person.

I decided to do the interviewing personally for five powerful reasons:

1. The interviews would give me an unparalleled opportunity to meet Canadian people and get the feel for the Canadian market (the interviews were scheduled for Toronto and Montreal).
2. I would personally be assured that no potentially capable candidate would "slip by" unrecognized.
3. I would get the feel of the salary situation in Canada.
4. From discussions with applicants, I would gain better insight into Canadian businesses, learn what others are doing, etc.
5. I would make each candidate feel special— knowing that a top company executive considered it worthwhile to see him or her personally.

We also resolved not to tell the applicants what we wanted or what we expected, but to learn from them just who they were, where they wanted to go, what they liked to do, what they would be capable of achieving.

The way to achieve this goal is to ask the right questions. Following is a brief list of "truth prodders" designed to produce the kind of information I have in mind.

Truth prodders

- What prompted you to apply to our company or to answer the ad in question?
- What, specifically, do you feel you could contribute to this particular company?
- What were your specific functions and responsibilities on your last job?
- What were the main factors that produced profits for your previous employer?
- What actions have you taken to contribute to the profit objective?
- What are some of the problems you ran into, and how did you solve them?
- What did you like best—and least—about your former job, the boss, the company?
- Were you satisfied with the way you were treated by the boss, the company? If, "Yes," then why did you leave? If, "No," in what ways were you treated unfairly?
- Here's a situation that came up in our plant (spell it out). What would you have done in this case?
- What are some of the techniques you use to train or develop people?
- Where would you like to be five or ten years from today and what income are you shooting for?

Get the idea?

I should mention that there were 40 interviews scheduled half an hour apart, on the hour and half-hour. How was I going to remember all those names and faces? Back then I had a Polaroid camera at my side. As

I interviewed each person, I snapped a picture so that when all 40 interviews were completed I had each person's resume, notes and picture to work from. Today, you can use your phone or tablet to store both their photos and your notes.

As the Mounties say, we "got our man." The extra time and effort really paid off.

12

GET TO THE POINT!

How many times have you read a letter that rambled on for pages before getting to the point or discussed a problem with someone who presented more explanations than specific proposals?

Why can't people get to the point?

I insist on two things in every memo I issue and every one I'm given to read: The main theme of the memo must be summed up in a sentence or two at the start; the work "action" must appear at the bottom—with the section itself clearly spelled out. This disciplines the writer to keep their thoughts on the beam. It sets the stage for fulfilling the memo's purpose quickly. And the reader gets the message fast.

One of our engineers who went out of town to look at a piece of equipment came back and wrote a beautiful two-page memo. After wading through it, I took a red pencil, wrote "so what" across it and promptly returned it.

The next day, I received a four-sentence memo from him. "This machine will do the job we want. It costs $5,000 delivered and installed. Based on production forecasts, we can save $5,000 in 14 months. I recommend we purchase the machine today; our vice president of manufacturing agrees." Action: I promptly approved the purchase.

Put stress on clarity

How many times have you thought "idiots" about a company because their catalog was fuzzy or their brochure didn't tell you what you wanted to know? Or, perhaps a set of assembly instructions struck you as senseless or confusing?

One time, our advertising and engineering departments issued a set of instructions for putting door frames together. They wrote the copy and an artist drew some cartoons.

I asked a friend of mine who happened to be in the office that day to try to put the frame together according to the instructions.

He couldn't.

Then I called in one of the accountants. But he, too, was "all thumbs."

So, we went down to the shop. Without giving him the instructions, I asked our master carpenter to install a door frame for us. Methodically and efficiently, he put the frame together.

I turned to the ad team and engineers. "People," I said, "that's the way it's done. Get that into your copy and cartoons."

13

DOES YOUR PARTNER HELP OR HINDER YOUR CAREER?

Given half a chance, your spouse or partner can help you develop and speed the savvy-building process. Or, if you don't watch out, it can work the other way. What it all boils down to is that the savvy manager will go farther faster if they are lucky enough to have a cooperative spouse or partner working with them—instead of against them.

The sympathetic partner can be a powerful career-booster.

The non-cooperative partner can be a powerful career-buster.

The fact is that whether your spouse or partner hinders or helps your career can depend as much on you as it does upon them. You both have to agree to deal with the events and the time that you plan to invest into your career.

Boosters or busters

In order to give you some idea of what I am talking about, I'll outline some common career-busting and career-boosting guidelines to follow. They're all quite simple, but ignore any of them and you could have problems—and not only domestic ones!

- The career-booster is willing to work at being charming—even when it hurts. They will smile throughout an evening even if deep down they want to sock-it-to-you...because it might affect the future for both of you.

- The career-booster learns to take the knocks with the benefits. Sometimes a business trip or special meeting conflicts with important social or family plans. More often than not, it can't be helped. That's why you're the manager. The career-buster grumbles and groans and is angry and bitter; the career-booster says, "I understand," even though it's not the easiest thing to say.

- The career-booster lets the driver drive, but the career-buster can become a "back-seat manager." A sympathetic spouse or partner is a natural sounding-board and hopefully a good listener, but a career-buster who relishes in being a "consultant" can unwittingly hinder your progress. An overly-ambitious spouse or partner can damage your career by pushing you into making rash decisions or, conversely, talk you out of transfers, promotions, etc.

- A career-booster can be the best PR advocate on the team. One time, my wife Phyllis and I took several distributors and their wives out to dinner. One couple was from Hawaii, so a trip to the States was a grand event for them. Phyllis sensed this and added to their holiday mood by making a special little fuss over them. Nothing obnoxious or obtrusive, but just enough to make them feel a little special. Multiply this by 40 or 50 other incidents involving customers, suppliers, business associates, community people and you can sense the important supplement to your managerial PR image a career-booster can be.

Rate yourselves

With this in mind, sit down with a pencil, a pad and your spouse or partner and discuss the career-boosters or career-busters bullets as honestly and objectively as you can. But keep in mind: When you rate them, you rate yourself at the same time. They can help you in many ways to thrust ahead in your career, but only if you help them to help you!

When you've completed the quiz, ask yourself this one final question: Are you still on speaking terms?

14

BLAST OUT OF YOUR SHELL

Got your sights on the executive suite, Mr./Ms. Engineer, Mr./Ms. Accountant or Mr./Ms. whatever your job specialty is? Well, you probably don't stand a chance of making it! Not a chance in the world.

It doesn't matter that you're the hottest person in your specialty. You're not going to hit the big-time, top management—unless you blast out of that narrow specialty of yours. I'm sure you spend a lot of time studying and practicing to become better in your field. Congratulations on getting as far as you have. But if you're perfecting your skills in one narrow area and <u>waiting</u> to be tapped for a broader management job, you'd better be the patient type. You've probably got a long wait ahead of you.

Where is it you want to go again? Top <u>management?</u> Does becoming a better and better <u>specialist</u> prepare you for <u>broad</u> management responsibilities?

Just the opposite. Specialists know a lot about a little. Managers know a little about a lot. Or even better, a lot about a lot.

Managers are people with the ability to take the <u>broad</u> view of things. Well then, how do you go about developing that type of "vision?"

You have to yank yourself out of your specialty. It's gotten you this far. But now you've outgrown it. To get into top management, you have to acquaint yourself with a broad range of business skills.

Talk to people in other fields. Or, more correctly, listen to people in other fields. Remember what one sage said: "There must be a good reason why man has only one mouth but two ears." Somehow, it's impossible to learn with your mouth open.

Read. Not just things that appeal to you. You've been doing that all your life. Read about things you've never been interested in. Read about things you know you really should have a better understanding of.

Here's a reading tip. Go to managers in other departments of your company. Find out from them the best journals, magazines and books in their fields. If some of what you read isn't clear, ask them. You'll not only get your question answered; you'll make some fast friends by showing interest in their line of work.

Do things you have never done before. For example, if you've avoided the opera because you thought you wouldn't like it, make a point of going to one or more performances. If you don't like it, at least you really <u>know</u> you don't. And perhaps opera will be to your liking after all.

In short, the idea is to do everything you can to break out of your well-ordered routine.

Time after time, people came to us at Steelcraft and said, "I want to be a foreman" or "I'd like to be plant superintendent" or "My ambition is to be a draftsman." They always seem to have their slots picked out.

Far too few said: "I want to find out how you do things here. I want to <u>learn</u> and <u>grow</u> with the business."

How refreshing that is to hear! All industry is crying for people like that. Are you such a person?

15

GETTING THE MOST OUT OF MEETINGS

Just about everybody's down on business meetings these days. They're generally regarded as a bore and a time waster. The meeting has even become the butt of jokes: "The camel is an animal designed by a committee."

Well, I disagree with all of this. Meetings can be a powerful communications pool. If they're not, the fault lies, not with some basic flaw in the meeting format, but in the way they're run.

Or more correctly—<u>not run</u>. That's the big problem with meetings: they're not properly led. Most of them wander all over the place like a leaf blowing in the wind.

There must be a specific purpose for every meeting. If there isn't, there shouldn't be a meeting in the first place.

Here's a tip on starting a meeting off on the right track. Have the leader clearly and succinctly state the purpose of the meeting at the beginning. Then, no one has an excuse for wandering afield of the reason for the meeting.

Without a good leader, a meeting will quickly deteriorate into a rambling, ponderous time waster. It only takes one person to switch it off onto a meaningless side track. It's the leader's job to drag it back on center, back to the purpose for which it was originally called.

Everybody has been at meetings that got badly off course. I remember one where the leader did a good job of

44

redirecting it back to target: One of our distributors had asked us to meet with him to discuss ways to train his team to do the final assembly work on our steel door frames and doors. It started out all right, but someone brought up a question on the way we package for shipment. Then, that reminded someone else about a question they had on why we use a particular trucking company.

At that point the chairman stepped in. "These questions you've just raised are good ones," he said. "But they're just a little off the subject we're here to discuss. I'll make a note to bring them up at a later date. Now, we were talking about training our team by ..."

Without offending anyone, he got the meeting headed back in the right direction. He also noted some matters that were worthy of discussion—but not at that moment.

Later, when I complimented him on his ability to run a meeting, he said: "It's like steering a boat. There are a number of things that can get you off course. You have to be constantly attentive to keep headed where you want to go."

And, <u>where you want to go</u> is a firm decision on what is to be done and who's to do it. This is where I use a very effective technique: I ask the person most affected by the decision to outline for the group the proposed action. It's then a matter of record that they understand what's to be done.

Their summation also serves to wrap up the meeting on a strong and forward-looking note that gives everyone involved the feeling that something has indeed been accomplished.

Here's one way to take the routine out of meetings: Don't always announce them in advance. What an unannounced meeting does is:

- Peaks interest. A special meeting? What's up?

- Yields off-the-cuff reactions that can often be very instructive. Sometimes "deep thought" just muddies things up.
- Trains people to think on their feet and sharpen their persuasive powers
- Pulls people out of their daily routine. This not only gives them a welcome breather; it often jars them out of routine thinking.
- Can pinpoint areas that weren't analyzed in sufficient depth.

And, to top it all, an unannounced meeting keeps the prevaricating out of the way so you get to the point quickly. Meetings are an effective management tool if they are well-run and if they are spiced with a little variety once in a while.

16

INVESTING IN YOURSELF

Now's a good time to talk investments. No, not the stock market type. I'm talking about a form of investing that's far more important than that—investing in <u>yourself</u>.

You want to get to the top, don't you? Not just your name on the door—I mean THE top. President. Chairman. Owner. The real big time.

If you're not aiming that high, you can stop reading right here. I'm talking to the men and women who have plans to make the heady climb all the way to the executive suite.

The fastest way to make that climb is by investing in yourself.

And, you do that by investing in your company. No, that's not double talk. Not when you realize that your advancement and your company's growth are all wrapped up together in a kind of partnership. Your part of the deal is to contribute everything you can to your company's success. For its part, your company is obliged to contribute as much as it can to your advancement.

What form does your contribution take? In a word: <u>sacrifice</u>. Think about it for a minute. That's what the owner does, doesn't he? That's what the top managers in your company do, don't they?

"If you want to be a success, act like the successful people do." That's old but good advice.

What sort of sacrifices? All sorts. I'll give you an example.

One of our managers at Steelcraft, let's call him Bob, had been working for months to close a big deal. The customer was ready to make a decision the last week in May and wanted Bob to come out to answer some final questions. It just so happens that Bob and his two sons were big auto racing fans and had been looking forward for a long time to take in the Indianapolis 500 on May 30. What's more, he and his family were planning to spend that last week in May with relatives in the Indianapolis area.

However, the contract in question was a good-sized one, and we were in neck-and-neck competition with other bidders. Without a single outward sign of disappointment, Bob cancelled his personal plans and followed through to a successful conclusion on the business deal.

Perhaps that's not the world's record sacrifice, but that vacation meant a lot to Bob. He knew, though, that he was the best one in the company to see that important deal through. And he was willing to act like top management— to sacrifice.

And you better believe we made it up to him. In the end, he wound up way ahead of the game.

But what if no one seems to appreciate your sacrifices? Suppose you make your sacrifices and the boss does not respond? What then? How long do you wait for the payoff to occur?

All right. We're being blunt. We're being realistic. Let us continue in this vein. How long do you wait? A reasonable length of time. How long is reasonable? That's hard to say. It varies from owner to owner, company to company. But that doesn't mean you invest of yourself wholeheartedly and with dedication entirely in the blind.

For one thing, there are signs to read. Watch others in the organization closely. Observe. Ask yourself, who else has been pouring their heart and gut into operation, and for how long? And what has been their reward? One thing you can almost surely count on—if others are being rewarded, you, too, will be taken care of in time—unless you're making the mistake of grossly overrating your efforts and abilities.

So, first and foremost, give of yourself. Never stop doing this, because it is the only way to build and sustain your growth. Then, wait patiently. Six months, a year, maybe longer. See how the wind is blowing. If you feel it's not blowing right for you, sit down and have a talk with your boss. Find out where you stand, where you're heading. Don't push or complain. Rather, put your cards on the table. Ask for advice and suggestions that will improve your effectiveness.

Then—and you're the only one who can do it—make your final judgment. But, try to be objective. Try to gauge your *true* value to your company, your *true* potential. Realistically. Without wishful thinking or blue-sky speculation. Then, face the issue squarely. Does it look like it's going to be all give, with little or no take? If so, this may be the time to move. The investment of yourself is too big, too overwhelmingly important, to be treated lightly or brushed aside.

And here's a tip: Should you decide to move, here's some advice: Do it fast. Don't lower the quality of your performance. This can only hurt you. There's absolutely nothing to be gained from sticking around. Quickly move on to some place where investing in yourself pays dividends.

17

SELL YOURSELF FIRST

I don't care what you're trying to sell, how good it is, how low priced—you still have to sell <u>yourself</u> first. That's the first step in any sale. Only after you've convinced your listener that you're someone to have confidence in can you even begin to direct his or her attention to your product or service.

Born salespeople know that instinctively. But I'm not just talking salespeople.

They're not the only ones involved in selling. Everyone is. Whatever your line of work—engineering, manufacturing, R & D—you're selling all day long.

<u>Savvy</u> managers realize this. They sell *themselves* to the people they manage <u>before</u> they try to sell their team on what they want done.

The best way to sell yourself is to prove your integrity and sincerity. Here's how:

- Be yourself. Try to be anything else and everyone will spot you for a phony. Leave acting for the pros who do it for a living.
- Accept criticisms of your product or ideas open-mindedly. If they're good ones, say so. Claiming infallibility invites suspicion.

- Don't simply hammer on the strong points and ignore possible flaws. If your listener brings them up, they'll be much harder to cope with. If you bring them up, the points your honesty scores can—and often does—outweigh the flaws.

- Flatter your listener. Most people can't resist something like: "You've got experience in this field. What do <u>you</u> think we should do?" Something like that will bolster his ego up several notches—guaranteed. And, he or she will be more favorably disposed to listen to what you have to say.

Now, here's a trick that all good salespeople use that you can put to work for you no matter what you're trying to sell: Prepare yourself for all possible objections to your product or idea.

How do you do this? My suggestion is to sit down with a pen and pencil and make a list of every selling hurdle, every objection you can think of. Really concentrate on putting yourself in your listener's shoes.

You'll find the objections will fall into one of four categories:

1. INVALID: <u>The simplest to overcome</u>. Your listener has been misinformed or somehow arrived at the wrong conclusion. Tactfully set the record straight. Making a big thing out of your being right and his being wrong may win your point —but will lose you the sale.

2. VALID: <u>A genuine disadvantage</u>. Don't try to brush aside real problems with your product or idea. Counter where you can with the compensating virtues. ("Yes. Putting on a shift

Saturdays and Sundays will mean considerable overtime expense, but the team has been asking for more overtime and it should give us a jump on the competition.")

3. VALID: <u>But you're working to eliminate them.</u> Point out what you are doing to correct these flaws.

4. VALID: <u>An objection you can turn to an advantage.</u> ("Using that heavier roller chain is going to cost more at first, but downtime will be reduced and it will outlast the chain we're now using 2.5 to 1. So, in the long run, switching will result in sizable savings.")

With this list of possible objections—and most importantly—your counters to them, you stand a good chance of winning the day, no matter what you want to sell and no matter who you are trying to sell it to.

One last sales pointer: With just about every listener, you have to establish your credentials as someone worth listening to. He or she is going to be thinking: "Why should I listen to <u>this</u> person talk about this subject? What's their special expertise in <u>this</u> field?"

The way to establish yourself as an "expert witness" is to do it in an offhand manner. <u>Quietly</u> point out your credentials—schooling, special training, years of experience, whatever.

<u>Quietly</u> is the key word here. Only the insecure little people feel they must strut like peacocks. Real experts don't feel the need to.

18

SHOOTING DOWN TROUBLES

Talk to most managers, and sooner or later they start to complain about their troubles. Profits down. Labor difficulties. Incompetent subordinates. Unreasonable customers. The list goes on and on...

I simply can't understand all the chronic complainers of the business world. What do they expect? For everything to run trouble-free with machine-like precision?

If it did, they'd be out of a job. Troubleshooting and problem-solving is what managers exist for. It's what they should thrive on. Did you ever look at it this way?

If there weren't any problems, there wouldn't be any such thing as business. Every single business opportunity is really the solution to some problem. The problems solved by such common things as computers, electric lights, rulers and lawn mowers, for example, provide business opportunities for thousands of companies.

The good manager, the savvy manager, concentrates much of his firepower on troubleshooting. But hitting the troubleshooting bull's eye takes a little practice and a little know-how.

Perhaps the most effective bit of ammunition in the expert troubleshooter's arsenal is the ability to look at things from someone else's point of view. Walk in the other person's shoes. Sit in their chair. Climb into their skin. No matter how it's popularly put, it means the same thing.

How do you acquire this all-important skill? I wish I could pass on an easy, fast-acting formula. But, there isn't one. The only one I know is <u>constant</u> practice. And <u>constant</u> means that you really work at switching places with everyone you talk to. Why everyone?

When it comes right down to it, everyone is just about equally important to you. The boss may be the one who okay's your raise, but your subordinates' good performances help you get it. Your customers are very, very important, of course. But, so are your suppliers, whose on-time deliveries make customer-pleasing easier.

So, no matter with whom you're talking—competitors, superiors, associates and so on—practice this: Practice the knack of gauging their answers to your questions from their position. When fully developed, this skill will give you invaluable insights into why others do what they do.

Let me give you an illustration: A new employee was assigned to your department several months ago. Ever since, the employee has muffed most of the assignments. Doing only half of what was asked. Missing deadlines. Misinterpreting the assignment altogether.

Why? Does he or she have some sort of weakness? Are they not up to the work? Do they have a problem that is diverting their full attention from the job?

Or, perhaps the problem lies with you? Looking at things from their point of view, are your instructions clear? Or, maybe, are you expecting that employee to pick up too much too quickly?

Talk to the employee about it. Drop leading questions. The only place you'll find the answer is in the other person's mind.

Another troubleshooting technique: Wipe out any potential misunderstanding as soon as it comes to light. For example, I re-read all the important letters I write. As I do, I listen to every sentence with this question constantly in my mind: "How could the reader take that the wrong way?" Every day, I catch something that could turn into a big, troublesome misunderstanding.

Here's a final troubleshooting hint: Once you've spotted trouble, zero in on the person most directly responsible for the problem area. Formulate a list of questions that strike to the heart of the problem. Call in the person and let fly with your questions.

Then there is just one thing left to do—retreat to a vantage point and watch that problem melt like an ice cube in boiling water.

19

SNIFFING OUT TALENT

More exciting than a fox chase; more fun than a scavenger hunt; and what a payoff: The Talent Hunt.

Savvy managers make it their business to snoop and sniff out hidden talent. It's one of the most rewarding of their pursuits.

Believe it or not, some so-called leaders are actually afraid to develop other people. They seem to feel threatened by the talents of others; they apparently fear they may be outclassed. That's a sign of a poor leader.

The really effective manager is constantly on the prowl for new talent.

One of our managers at Steelcraft was constantly developing outstanding people—and they had grown, they were frequently pulled out for strategic jobs in other departments. But did he mind? Not a bit. He put the interests of the company first, and knew that he was making a valuable contribution. Also, he really enjoyed seeing the people he worked with develop and grow in ability and responsibility. Meanwhile, he grew with them—impressively—in both pay and position. His worth was recognized and appreciated.

To start a talent hunt program, where do you begin? What do you look for? Which of your people is most likely to possess the hidden potential that could mean so much to them—and to you?

Well, there is no clear-cut, scientific approach to the recognition of talent, for it is immeasurable. But, there are a few pretty good clues you might look for:

- Your talented employee is probably a prober, a searcher, a questioner, with a thirst for knowledge.
- They won't blindly accept the current way of doing things. They have their own ideas and challenge existing methods.
- They won't accept orders routinely and without thought. They are not belligerent, but they do want to know the <u>why</u> of things.
- They don't like to be idle. They get restless and dissatisfied if they don't have enough to do. If they're caught up on their own work, they'll often volunteer to help others.

There's nothing foolproof about these clues; they are just that—clues. But they're pretty good ones, and a person who fills the entire bill is a person to be watched, trained, developed.

The effective talent sniffer takes the time to review the lower-level jobs to flush out people with spunk, with ideas and imagination. One time, I dropped in on a production meeting—just snooping around. It was on the line- and supervisory-level. A discussion was in progress, and Jim K., a production man, was speaking. I didn't want to be a distraction, so I quietly sat down at the rear of the room and listened carefully to what he had to say.

It didn't take me long to discover that Jim had the answer to a problem that had baffled others for some time.

I liked the way he presented his ideas; I also liked the way he listened when another view was presented.

I left quietly with the feeling that my small investment in time would reap a handsome dividend.

A successful talent scout must keep a sharp eye on the "quarry," observe their actions, their method of thinking and planning over a period of time. Get to know them not only as a worker, but as a person.

Jim K. didn't know it, but he was under close scrutiny. Shortly after my visit to the production meeting, I mentioned his name to our manufacturing manager, who had also noticed Jim's potential. It wasn't long before there was a special project for Jim on which the young team member could really test his skills. Jim was well on his way, as we began informally developing his talents, fortifying his strengths, shoring up his weaknesses.

Jim is an exception. Outstanding talent is always an exception. But the really savvy manager will also be challenged by an employee who doesn't quite fill the bill, who doesn't seem to provide every one of the clues we listed a moment ago.

The employee may, after all, be talented but also timid. Their hidden potential may be so deeply hidden it would take a derrick to bring it to the surface. Well, that derrick is you, their savvy manager.

It is you who can motivate that person, inspire and encourage them. Explore their interests, invite their opinions, build their self-confidence.

It won't happen often, but every once in a while, you will uncover a talent that will repay your efforts again and again. And that is the supreme achievement.

How about sitting down with a pencil and paper today to list some names?

Run each and every subordinate through those four clues a talent scout should look for. It's a cinch you'll come up with some good sources of untapped talent.

In fact, there's a reserve of untapped talent in every one of us. Our job is to learn just how deeply the reserve is hidden within ourselves and within each of the people we are directly responsible for.

Then the thing to do is ... start tapping.

20

THE ART OF AGITATION

If you'd like to be a savvy manager, here's a rule to follow: Spend half your time developing yourself and the other half developing your subordinates.

Your goal is to be a high-powered, self-starting go-getter, right? Well, as a manager, it's part of your job to instill that same attitude in your subordinates. It's not easy. But it pays off—not only for your company, but for you, too.

How so? Remember that you, Savvy Manager, are judged not only on how well <u>you</u> do, but also on how well <u>everyone</u> reporting to you does. The better they perform, the better you look.

All right then, how do you spark your people into action? In a word: AGITATE. It's one of the most powerful weapons in the savvy manager's arsenal.

Agitate can mean steering your people into new avenues of thought. Take this example: One of the accountants at Steelcraft—let's call him George—was doing an excellent job, with one exception.

George concentrated on nothing but accounting. He came in early, worked hard all day and often stayed late. But outside the accounting department, he was lost. He not only didn't know what most of the other departments did; he hardly even knew where they were.

I couldn't let that continue.

One day, when George and I had finished discussing a budget study he had done, I asked, "How would you like to come with me on my daily plant walk-through?"

I could see the idea didn't exactly excite him, but, of course, he couldn't turn down an invitation from the boss.

I told him that we weren't simply on a "goodwill" tour. This daily walk-through was one of my ways of keeping track of what was going on.

"George, if I just sat back in my office and waited for people and reports to come to me, I'd never keep up with things in this company. In fact, we like to see all of our people get out of their departments once in a while to take a look around the operation."

The suggestion wasn't lost on George. And a couple of weeks later, this suggestion paid off for our company.

On one of his newly established "plant tours," George noticed that some of the crew touched up the paint on some of the doors we manufactured using the small aerosol paint cans that we furnished to customers as a service.

George, having an accountant's mind, suspected that this was an expensive way to take care of touch-up work. He checked with our purchasing department, and found that each pint aerosol can cost 75 cents. A gallon, eight times as much paint, cost $4.50, or only six times as much as a pint. George immediately brought this to the attention of the right person, and this profits leak was plugged. With all the painting we did, George's suggestion amounted to a nice savings over a year's time.

So, that's the end of that. George saved the company some money, but that's what every employee is supposed to do. Nothing out of the ordinary, right?

No, that is not the end. It is unlikely that either George or any other employee will keep producing for you without one essential ingredient that you, the savvy manager, must add: Recognition.

It can be a handshake, a nod, a notice on the bulletin board, a savings bond. It can take any form. The important thing is that it is given.

Thomas Fuller once said, "They that value not praise will never do anything worthy of praise." It's a rare person who doesn't appreciate, even crave, recognition.

So engrave the word RECOGNITION high on your management savvy list.

21

YOUR PERSONAL LIFE IS AN ASSET

Savvy-building is not a nine-to-five job. Skilled savvy managers develop off-the-job techniques which strengthen their business skills. Basically, they expand their management abilities to include: (a) their family, (b) their community, and (c) their personal living habits.

I have no patience with the go-getter who is in the office regularly at the crack of dawn and never leaves for home until nine or ten o'clock. I do not happen to think that the longer the day, the better the manager.

Successful savvy managers get others to do things for them. They guide, train, direct and develop talent, and then they are free for more important, innovative tasks.

Sure, I know that the manager as a person with responsibility has more demands on their time than many other people. There will be an occasional trip out-of-town, a late evening, maybe even a weekend business session. But 11 or 12 hours a day adds up to family neglect, and this can be almost as harmful to a manager as business neglect.

For your family needs your management expertise as well. I recently came across a 12-year old's impression of a happy family: "A happy family is like a team—Mom pitching, Dad catching and the kids fielding—with everyone taking a turn at bat."

In our home, we liked to give everyone a turn at bat. When I was confronted with a situation involving important social and business conflicts, I called upon my savvy to solve the problem:

My wife and I were expected to attend an important charitable event, but I was expecting a very important telephone call from someone on-the-road who couldn't be reached at any other time. He needed to receive instructions from me that would prevent headaches later.

What could I do? I couldn't be in two places at one time. I turned to my 15-year-old son, Jon, and asked if he would be able to handle the telephone call. He was eager to help. So, we sat down and I gave him the full instructions on what to do; then my wife and I left for our engagement.

When we arrived home, Jon's buttons were popping! The call had come through, the instructions were given, and everything was all right. The next day I talked to the caller, who complimented me on the way my son had handled the call! "That boy of yours is a real pro!" Now it was **my** turn to pop buttons!

Become actively involved in the affairs of your community and follow through on your commitments. You'll become a local hero and serve your own ends at the same time! Here again, the multiple value concept comes into play. The community gains; you gain, too.

The payoff comes in a variety of ways. For example, community service sharpens your organizational abilities; smooths your personality's rough spots; helps you handle responsibility with greater assurance; hones motivational skills; cultivates your speaking abilities; develops you into a "master evaluator;" builds the idea-generating habit.

Well-rounded managers live a well-balanced life. They sleep enough, but not too much. They drink in moderation most of the time. Their chief overriding interest is <u>people</u>. They are concerned with how people act and react. They know that only <u>with</u> people and <u>through</u> people can their life be rich and rewarding—both on and off the job.

Savvy managers get around and involve themselves in all sorts of problems. They evaluate judgments and decisions from various points of view. As part-lawyer, part-clergyman, part-entertainer, they are constantly on display.

Keep this last point in mind. Don't fog up your personal public relations mirror with a singular image—the office "wolf," the "wise-guy," the "bookend." Keep in mind all your adverse characteristics by answering the following questions:

1. <u>How do I look to others</u>? Like it or not, appearance means a lot to some people. Do I look, act and feel clean? Am I in good shape? Do I dress neatly?

2. <u>Am I a good listener</u>? The person who can listen appreciably to a story or idea is in great demand.

3. <u>Do I talk too much</u>? Chances are that the windbag will not go too far. Almost assuredly they are a bore, a project stopper, a production stumbling block.

4. <u>Do people think of me as the "character?"</u> Any characteristic that subtracts from the respect you command hinders you; keep that in mind the next time you play a practical joke.

5. <u>Am I a good-goody, super-virtuous loyalist</u>? To put it more bluntly, are you the teacher's pet? If you are, shape up.

6. <u>Am I myself</u>? The person who makes the biggest hit on or off the job is the one who acts naturally and unpretentiously.

7. <u>Am I "easy to get along with</u>?" Everyone enjoys the company of a pleasant, friendly person. The one who argues, who's the perpetual dissenter, triggers resentment.

8. <u>Do I wear a "smile on my umbrella</u>?" A warm, friendly smile—not put on—has magical appeal. It draws people out, makes them respond.

9. <u>Am I overaggressive</u>? Ambition that is too apparent or carried to extremes can be self-defeating.

10. <u>Am I true to my role as manager</u>? The urge to be "one of the gang" can be strong. Be a "regular person," by all means, <u>but never at the expense of your people's respect</u>.

22

CUSTOMER SERVICE WORKS!

It's the best, easiest and cheapest way to build a successful business, yet some companies still treat customers as an inconvenience.

It's time you became an obsessed manager—but don't be concerned. This isn't any unhealthy obsession. On the contrary, this obsession is essential. It centers around giving the best possible service to customers—be they clients or other departments in your company. This obsession is important, because it ultimately lies at the heart of any company's success. Customer service is a lost art. In fact, I'm surprised when I do get good service. Some friends tell me that they no longer expect to be treated with special attention or even courtesy when they take their car to be serviced, deal with a store clerk or visit a medical facility.

The attitude today seems to be that the customer is an inconvenience, a necessary evil to be dealt with as perfunctorily as possible. This is a shame for both the seller *and* the buyer.

From the seller's point of view, good customer service is the best and easiest way to build a successful, growing business. I have stressed customer service all through my career—first as owner of a manufacturing company, then as an executive in a large company, and then as the owner of three hotels in Florida. Customer service works! It is in the businessperson's own self-interest to stress service to the customer, because customers are getting short-changed.

Simple consideration

Here's how we attracted one customer to one of my hotels:

He sold electronic gear that was too valuable to leave in his car overnight and too cumbersome to move by hand. In other hotels, when he had asked to borrow a bellhop's cart, he was refused. Each time he wanted his equipment moved, he had to call the desk and have the bellhop bring the cart.

When he checked into our hotel, we gave him a bellhop's cart with his name on it. It was his to use for the duration of his stay. He was a happy guest, kept coming back, and told others about us. He also told us he still couldn't get this kind of simple, individual consideration at other hotels.

Customer service works. It is easy. It costs little or nothing. It puts money in the till. It makes both giver and receiver feel good.

Good customer service means putting the customer's interests first, bending over backwards, if necessary, to satisfy the customer and treat customers individually, according to their needs.

Poor customer service is treating customers with disdain, adhering to standard rules and policies at the expense of the customer's interests, and believing that the customer has no choice but to accept things as they are.

Part of the problem is the way business people are trained. Some time ago, I conducted a survey of 34 leading graduate schools and 56 highly ranked undergraduate schools. None had a curriculum that included a single program or course devoted to explaining the customer's role in the marketplace. At Lynn University in Boca Raton, where I am currently working, we teach a course in our hospitality department on customer service. Other colleges are cranking out graduates with administrative and technical skills and number shufflers well-versed in computer technologies—however these people lack in the basic tenets of customer and human relations.

Former Business Week editor-in-chief Lew Young states, "In too many companies, the customer has become a bloody nuisance whose unpredictable behavior damages carefully made strategic plans."

The Association of Better Business Bureaus stated that 23 percent of all customer complaints were about unsatisfactory customer service. Another seven percent concerned unsatisfactory service on repair jobs.

According to a survey by a Washington D.C.-based research firm, the average company does not hear from 96 percent of its unhappy customers. Between 65 and 90 percent of these non-complainers stop doing business with the supplier. Yet, the same survey reports that 54 to 70 percent of complainers can be won back simply by resolving their problems.

Days gone by

I dealt with a Florida bank for 16 years. As the owner of three large hotels and other enterprises in the area, my account was fairly substantial. For 10 years, I had borrowed money on a short-term cycle, repaying it promptly each year. One day, the bank was bought out by a holding company, one of the biggest. With the new ownership, new rules were introduced. My line of credit was suddenly questioned. I discussed the situation with the executive vice president in charge of the company, and his response: "Sorry, the days of the local, friendly banker are gone." Also gone was a customer of 16 years.

How could *anyone* not understand that good customer relations adds up to good business? We must battle insensitivity to customers on two fronts—the corporate and the academic. Since the academic world is the preliminary training ground for executives-to-be, it is here that the importance of customer service must be explained. Every successful and outstanding company I have ever dealt with is customer-sensitized and headed by a chief executive literally driven on the subject of providing exceptional service.

'Zonked out'

When I was in the hotel business, our key operational word (courtesy of Peters and Waterman) was "OBSESSION." My aides and employees—from executive vice president to busboy—considered met a nut on the subject of customer relations. This was precisely the image I wished to convey. I am admittedly zonked out on the concept. I contend that caring obsessively about my customers and their feelings kept the organization flourishing and the payroll met. Business was conducted on two levels. Level One deals with the matters of marketing, finance and statistical analysis in which the computer figures so prominently. A businessperson would be a fool to understate the importance of these functions. They are vital parts of the corporate body. But these Level One parts would be of no value without the parts of Level Two.

Level Two involves people—employees, suppliers, the public and customers. And, the most important people to the corporate goal and mission are the company's customers—what they want, what they need, how they feel and how they react. The overriding failure of today's economy is the excessive corporate emphasis on technical and analytical aspects as compared to the human and personal aspects.

No interest?

Perhaps the most logical and significant explanation for the breakdown of customer service is what psychiatrists sometimes call "the principle of least interest." As we travel down the wage-and-rank totem pole, the employees' stake in the business, and what makes it successful, tends to diminish. Employees must be convinced that good customer relations is in their best personal interest and will protect their jobs. This job of convincing must be a top priority of chief executive officers and their closest aides. The chief executive needs to generate continuing awareness of the importance and need for top quality customer orientation.

Obsession with service is not a once-in-a-while state of mind; it is now and forever. Regardless of how busy you may be on other matters, sit down periodically with your key decision-making people to get this message across and make sure it isn't forgotten. Hold discussion sessions with the specific goal of improving customer service. Memos addressing this subject should be constantly flowing back and forth. About once a month, I held 20-minute orientation meetings to impress on new employees the urgency of superior customer service. This set their thinking straight from the start.

Now is the time for the corporate and academic communities to join forces. America has long been a world leader in technology, and the business schools have been at the forefront of innumerable "breakthroughs." What is missing is feeling.

H.J. Zoffer, dean of the University of Pittsburgh's Graduate School of Business, is an educator alert to, and aware of, this problem. He says: "We need a way to reach the spirit, develop the nerve and create the need for venturing to light the fire of creativity in our students so they understand the difference between administering and managing." Indeed, such a restructuring and readdressing of the success elements in the marketplace would greatly enhance corporate bottom-line results, as well as cause countless customers and consumers to cheer.

23

DEVELOPING YOUR TEAM

Winston Churchill achieved world renown as one of the greatest leaders of modern times. But without the British people and the British military behind him, we might never have heard his name.

Lovable, rambunctious Casey Stengel won immortality for himself in Baseball's Hall of Fame as pilot of the first team in history to take five pennants in a row. But without the scintillating performance of the New York Yankees of the forties and fifties, Casey might be a comparative unknown today.

David Merrick's skill and sensitivity as a gifted director made his name a byword in the theatrical world. But without the talent and drive of the men and women who worked under him, no outlet for his genius would exist.

In business, in government, in politics, in sports—or anywhere else—if you're a manager, you succeed through your people!

The formula is clear-cut. First, pick the right people. Next, identify and tap their abilities. Finally, build their abilities, then channel them towards the achievement of profit goals. The point is that no matter how smart you are, how well-educated, ambitious, personable, enthusiastic and conscientious—you succeed through your people.

Track down natural leaders and let them lead

How well your people on the line perform will depend largely on the quality of inspiration and guidance provided, not only by yourself, but by their close and immediate managers.

Your selection and development of these key people, more than any other single factor, will determine your personal reputation and growth. I'm talking about your sub-leaders. There are two kinds of managers in business today:

1. THE NATURAL LEADER: A pleasant individual, they are friendly, interesting, personable. You're warmed by their smile, and provoked by their style. There's something about them. They exude confidence. You get the feeling that they are in control of the situation. Were they born this way or did they develop along these lines? You can argue this one at length. It's no matter. The stuff is there. The feeling is real.

2. THE APPOINTED LEADER: They may be the most able person in the world. Or a ho-hum character. Cheerful and amiable. Or cranky and cantankerous. Exciting or dull. They may be holding down their job because of seniority, because of a special skill they possess, because of a giant-sized mistake that somebody made. Whatever the reason, they are there. Appointed. In charge of a division, a department, a group.

Now, what is the ideal mix for you, as a savvy manager, to seek? Let me give you one example: A young fellow,

Bill, worked for us. He was in his early thirties. Bill's eyes spark with personality. Sharp, easy to work with, he automatically inspires cooperation. Bill has plenty to crow about. But you never hear him crowing. His actions crow for him. Bill is a natural leader. Something to think about: Bill started as a rank and-filer. He was promoted to manager. Then he became a department head.

Not by accident, but by design

How come? Because Bill likes people, and people like him. He motivates them. He inspires them. He gets them to respond. Bill scores high on what Walter Lippmann referred to as "the final test of a leader" that I feel is so important. He "leaves behind him in other men the conviction and will to carry on."

Once again, what ideal should you shoot for? You do your utmost to make the natural leader the appointed leader. You tie the two together wherever you can.

How to pick a winner: Chemical reactions

There was a service company in our area whose management team worked well together. They understood and respected one another. At one point, a new promotion manager was hired who was capable and experienced, with an excellent background. There was no apparent reason why he shouldn't have made the grade.

But he didn't make the grade.

The new man wasn't a snob exactly. But the rest of the team sensed a too-patrician bearing about him, an almost imperceptible superciliousness of manner.

Or maybe it was their imagination?

In any case, he didn't last. The team was unable to accept him on comfortable terms. After four weeks he resigned.

The reason? It would be difficult to explain in concrete terms.

But, here's what I always maintain: I believe that for people to work well together, there must be a kind of chemistry between them. It may be forced to begin with, but after a certain period of association it must become natural.

I think it's important in selecting your people to keep sharply aware of this chemical reaction. In today's business organization, people from all walks of life are thrown together. Their values, their hopes and their aims may vary. Their family background, their upbringing, their accustomed economic levels may be different.

Still, to function efficiently as a smoothly operating, profit-minded team, an agreeable blend must be established, a common understanding and acceptance achieved. I call this "Chemical Response-ability." And I believe that as a savvy manager, you cannot do your compounding too carefully. As I mentioned in Chapter 11 on hiring your team, all it takes is a single wrong element to dilute and weaken the formula. The trick is to project yourself into the minds of your people.

How to shake the cart without spilling the apples

One time, we needed a manager in the engineering department. Our normal policy was to bring people up from within to fill key jobs, but we were in a period of explosive growth and had advanced as many people as we could at that particular time.

So we scouted the field, and found a person interested in joining our organization who currently held the top engineering post in a smaller company.

Now I don't have to tell you that when you bring in a key person to supervise other people you're treading on delicate ground. For one thing, you risk a serious morale flare-up. Some people will be upset that they didn't get the job. Another thing is while that any employee in a new job is on trial, so to speak, a manager is doubly on trial. The manager who is also an outsider has all the chips stacked against them—unless you take positive steps to unstack them. That's exactly what we did in this case.

Here's a step-by-step rundown of the "reverse interview" strategy we used:

1. We permitted our chosen person to be interviewed by some of the people who would be working under him. He was not interviewed in the usual sense. We did nothing to dilute his authority as a manager, or to undermine our own management prerogatives. We simply told our people we were thinking of hiring this individual. We encouraged them to speak with him and let us know how they felt he would fit into our organization. This made them feel important and included. It offset the effect of having an unpopular management action thrust down their throats.

2. We had each of our people report their findings to us. Though most were guardedly cautious, it helped pave the way to ultimate acceptance.

3. When we made known the addition to our organization, we announced other changes at the

same time. This helped to offset and minimize the major change.

4. We worked up some popular innovations for the new person to initiate. By having him announce the innovations himself, he was regarded as either the author of—or at least a strong campaigner for—the moves.

5. We played up his image of professional achievement. We publicized his former top engineering post, his awards and published work.

6. Most importantly, we went out of our way to give him our fullest cooperation. We made every effort to implement his ideas without delay.

Why all this rigmarole over one man? We could easily have announced the mandate: "This is our new person. He will be your boss. You will carry out his orders, or else!"

The reason is clear. That's not the way we did things. My theory is that you don't command when you can convince.

The Result: This man's career with us was distinguished by outstanding success and his department was one of the most productive in the company.

Practice "people-ized talent exploitation"

As a savvy manager, your prime objective is to expand your span of control, to multiply the number of profit actions you take in a given period of time. As the poet Schlegel says: "Every enterprise begins with and takes its first step in faith."

But faith doesn't just happen. You work with and through people to develop it. The extent to which you succeed in having this blind faith in your people testifies to the effectiveness of your training ability.

If at first they don't succeed—teach, teach again

Directly or indirectly, savvy managers spend 75 percent of their time guiding and instructing people. This doesn't have to be a formalized procedure:

- Training is more often a matter of exposing people to right ways of doing things. They learn by osmosis.
- If your people respect you, they will imitate you. They will follow in your footsteps much faster than they will follow your advice.
- The best way to solve a problem is to break it down into bits and pieces and analyze it in depth.

Here's a live example based on that premise: In this particular case, we had an order handling problem. We had set up a scheduling system in the plant, and it wasn't working right. So I called a meeting. My multiple-value goal was not only to get this scheduling problem solved, but to sharpen the problem-solving ability of my people. The problem-solving objective was to meet a three- or four-week delivery schedule, regardless of quantity ordered and other factors involved.

I kicked off the meeting by asking to have the system defined.

An order department supervisor took the floor. "Well," he began, "an order comes in and we process it. Then it goes to the ..."

I interrupted. "What do you mean, it 'comes in?' Where does it come from? Which desk does it go to? How long does it stay there? What does the processing consist of?"

Step by step. Every detail accounted for. Depth analysis. But I didn't do it for him; I goaded him into doing it for himself.

That's what I mean by training. It's not preaching. It's not lecturing. It's guiding and goading. It's organizing and directing, individual therapy and group therapy.

I rode hard on those employees. I chewed them out. I laced into them. What I really did was unite them. Six people all driven by the boss. They teamed together in their common misery—and they loved it. They also learned.

Detail by detail the system started shaping up; just what I was waiting for. The group began to carry on by themselves. My job was done. Off I went to expand my span of control.

Training—there's nothing cut and dried about it

Training is a highly individual process. Each manager has his or her own way of teaching. Each trainee has their own way of learning. One person will respond to pressure, another to a well-presented challenge, a third to a carefully calculated vanity prod. The idea is to experiment. Vary your strategy until you find the one that works best for each person.

On one of my people, for example, I used this strategy. "Joe," I'd say, "the trade show mix-up is giving us a lot of trouble, what do you think would be the best way to handle it?" Joe, flattered that the boss wants his opinion, went all out to study the problem. And, he usually came up with a good solution.

It's the old story. The effectiveness of your training program boils down to the question of how well you can motivate the participation of your people.

As N.J. Berrill points out in "Man's Emerging Mind:" "A great teacher is not simply one who imparts knowledge to his students, but one who awakens their interest in it and makes them eager to pursue it for themselves. He is a spark plug, not a fuel pipe."

Your job as a teacher is to start the engine running. Once this is done, the "distribution system" will usually take care of itself.

Compile your personal checklist of "response factors"

As I pointed out, how a person will respond to a training motivator is unpredictable if you go about it on a guesswork basis. One person needs a shot in the arm, another, a shot in the ego. That's why a reliable inventory of "Response Factors" will make your training job a great deal easier. Such a checklist is easy to compile. You start by writing down every training motivational strategy that comes to mind. Pressure. Challenge. Ego feeding. Promotion bait. Appeal to special talent or interest. Plus others of your own that you have tried or might try.

Next, write the name of all your people on a sheet of paper. Alongside each person's name enter the motivators that work best for them. Finally, experiment. Learn about your people. Try all your strategies on all your people. Then, all you have to do is pinpoint the ones that work best.

"People-ize" your firing strategy, too

You might as well face one fact: All the management savvy in the world won't make you infallible. No matter how much skill you apply in the selection and development of your people, you are going to make mistakes from time to time. Weaknesses will crop up in people that neither you nor they are able to overcome. Or, the growth of an individual may not keep pace with the growth of their job.

Whatever the reason, at one time or other you are going to be faced with the miserably distressing job of having to fire one of your people.

Distasteful as this is—and I can think of no management task that is more onerous—firing one of your staff can have its positive side, too. If the job is done properly, it can be constructive and beneficial for your subordinate and yourself. But it takes a special kind of skill and savvy to "people-ize" your firing strategy.

Positive value from a negative task

It's difficult to fire anyone. But take a person with twelve years in the company, who walks with a limp, and the task is one that can haunt you at night. That situation fit one employee—we'll call him Jack—who had a chronic attendance problem. He was often absent, more often late. We spoke to him about it repeatedly. He promised to change, but the promise was never fulfilled.

Attendance was Jack's biggest problem, but not his only problem. His attitude was worse than poor. He gave the impression that he didn't like people, and they responded in kind.

We tried everything: warnings, discussion, job variety, special challenges. Nothing worked. Finally, we ran out of solutions and there was only one solution left. We had to let him go.

All right. Here's where the "people-ized" firing strategy comes into the picture. To set the framework, here are the seven key points that comprise the technique:

1. Clearly establish the reason for the firing action, and prove the fairness and justice of your decision.
2. Give the person a chance to have their say and present their side.
3. Use your persuasive powers to help straighten the person out, so that they will have a greater chance to succeed at their next job.
4. Inject a positive note. Stress their abilities and strengths. Show them how the change will benefit them in time to come—they might get a much better job.
5. Play up and dramatize their "bird-in-the-hand" severance benefits.
6. Wish them luck. Convince them of your genuine interest in their welfare and future.
7. Reinforce your show of concern by expressing your willingness to help them should they need it in the future.

People-ized team building round-up tips

1. Here's a thought to take with you and come back to at regular intervals: You succeed through your people. Any uncorrected weaknesses they possess,

any undeveloped talent, is an obstacle in your path to success, as well as theirs.

2. Try where you can to appoint natural leaders to key spots in your department. The appointed natural inspires cooperation. People instinctively turn to them for direction and guidance.

3. A tuba player and a piccolo player would render a weird duet. For people to play or work well together, the ingredients of their character and personality must blend. Orchestrate!

4. If you have to go outside of your company to fill a key post, proceed with extreme caution. Don't drop the newcomer like a bomb among your people. Ease them in gradually. Take definite steps to encourage their acceptance and build respect for their professional competence.

5. The small company employee often has an exceptional chance to grow. They "rub elbows" with the boss, have top management attention called to their talents, get in on challenging tasks and decision-making responsibilities and achievements. If you're a small company manager, use this persuasive selling argument in the recruitment of key people.

6. Expand your span of control by developing blind faith in your people. Use "people-ized" techniques to exploit their talents. Work with them and through them, build their strengths, shore up their weaknesses and tap their natural talents until you foster in them the ability to operate independently of your close surveillance and control.

7. Take stock of your "Personal Trust Fund." Analyze the degree of reliance you now place on each of

your people. Then take positive steps to strengthen their abilities and, as an automatic by-product, your trust.

8. Use the "Follow the Leader" development strategy. Show a person what to do and how to do it. Then get them to do what you've shown them. Repeat the process until it takes.

9. Motivation! It's the master key to people development. It's the launching pad of savvy management. Horace Mann puts it this way: "The teacher who attempts to teach without inspiring the pupil with a desire to learn is hammering on cold iron." So warm up that furnace. Stimulate. Inspire. Motivate!

10. Don't train your people in a ho-hum, routine fashion. Analyze their motivational "Response Factors." Find out what makes them want to learn.

11. "People-ize" your firing strategy. When forced to let a person go, keep three key questions in mind: (a) How can you help them? (b) How can you minimize the adverse morale effect of the firing on employees and the community? (e) What reasonable steps can you take to assure that you and the discharged employee part as friends, not enemies?

24

THAT MOMENT OF DECISION

There may come a time in life when you come face-to-face with a "moment of decision" on the critical issue involving your career and future. It may even happen more than once. In the future, how will we remember our decision? Will we consider how much our mental condition factored in? Were we under stress? Were we in a hurry? Had we really thought out the problem and made a logical and solid decision? My contention is that, too often, we are so emotionally involved that our decisions may be irrational.

"Moments of decision" should be handled under the most ideal conditions, with as much counseling and varied advice as possible. Remember that free advice from friends about a decision that you have to make and live with should always be taken with reservation, but, if, on the other hand, you talk to a variety of people and get the same general direction, then you can safely trust the "advice."

Listening to others

One of the dangers in talking to people about your career is that people often do not know enough about your situation to give you advice. They may be full of misinformation or offer you advice based on their own experiences, abilities and limitations. On the positive side, it does help to talk to people with whom you have respect to stimulate ideas that will aid you in your thinking process. By talking to other people, you can learn data that you might not have had in mind—but follow your instincts in the way you use the data.

In our survey of executives, I found that the majority like their existing jobs, although *half of them* might have made a *different choice* if they were to have had the chance. There were also some interesting comments made that some were afraid and not willing to accept more personal risk.

Your personal growth

One survey respondent said about a career decision, "I wish I had understood my gifts, abilities and potential as well at age 22 as I do now." Which brings to mind another major issue: Too often we underestimate our ability. We do not take time to review our talent and how it can play in any decision. We have to be careful not to overdo this idea, but only you know what you can and cannot do.

Perhaps we would all be better off making early career decisions with more knowledge of our skills and talents. One of the best ways to develop and learn about our abilities is to practice when we are young, which we can do by becoming involved in community activities and taking leadership roles in these avenues. We can also do this as we grow older—it's never too late! Many older people who get involved in non-profit organizations find new vistas of excitement and have new opportunities to learn leadership and team work. These new skills—at any age—can help bring success to an existing job or even an entirely new career.

It is interesting to see how people do change in their abilities and interests. It's like watching children who continually have different ideas, goals and aspirations. Perhaps that progress never stops, but continues forever. It's important to develop a liking for change, so that you become comfortable with it and not afraid of it. Take advantage of the opportunity for change, since that is how we expand our skills and abilities.

Nothing happens automatically in life. I believe you create the environment and put yourself in the situation for opportunities. You make the "breaks" by networking, making yourself available, being slightly aggressive and keeping your eyes open for chances.

If you continue your education, become involved in community life (which I call paying civic rent), stay involved in your children's and your spouse's activities and develop your communication skills, you will find that you will continue to grow internally, which will enable you to face unbelievable obstacles.

The past is the past ... let it alone

It is very hard to stop the mind from thinking back on decisions you have made in the past. This is especially true when you think about decisions that turned out to be bad ones. Keep moving forward.

25

WHAT AN EXECUTIVE SHOULD KNOW ABOUT THE ULTIMATE COMPETITIVE EDGE

An incredibly large number of high-level executives in today's marketplace could quite accurately state: "We have met the competition, and it is us."

The reason is that the primary service practiced by too many companies is lip service to customer service. It's like the weather; everyone talks about it, but that's about as far as it goes. However, if you pinpoint some of the brightest and most profitable stars of American enterprises and investigate the main reason for their success, in almost every case you will find it is because they know how to make customers happy and keep them that way.

Competition, when you boil it down and distill it, is people. And if your objective is to compete successfully, you can only do so by satisfying the most important people of all—the ones who buy your products or services—more effectively than your competitors. Simple as that may sound, on the typical list of executive and supervisory priorities, the Ultimate Competitive Edge (Superior Customer Service) doesn't even appear. In corporations and retail stores throughout the nation I have observed time and again that service is taken for granted.

How, precisely, does the Ultimate Competitive Edge work? For one thing, superior customer service goes a giant step beyond ordinary and conventional bottom line strategies. It goes beyond being friendly, polite and obliging. UCE is an aggressor's marketing weapon. It is a weapon you must train yourself to use, train the people who work for you to use, and you must inspect the troops constantly to make sure they never stop using it.

UCE's objective is to surprise customers so pleasantly it will make them sit up and take notice. In my experience, the trick in making this happen is to search for ways and means of achieving a level of service that comes off as so special and custom-tailored to the customer's needs and desires that it would never occur to him or her to do business elsewhere.

In striving for competitive superiority, I have found that certain critical operational words stand out: Uniqueness ... Imagination ... Dedication ... Resolution ... and most important of all, OBSESSION.

I readily admit I'm obsessed—a fanatic and nut on the subject of customer service. I will forgive all kinds of errors in my organization, but will under no circumstances tolerate second-rate service.

Obsession about customer service is for me the master key to success. More than a word, it is an emotional fixation!

I have found that whether it is a task force group, a department, division, corporation, conglomerate— whatever the shape or size of the work team—IF THE PERSON IN CHARGE IS OBSESSED ON THE SUBJECT OF SERVICE AND FOLLOWS THROUGH ON THAT OBSESSION, the Ultimate Competitive Edge will develop as an automatic byproduct of the leader's obsessive behavior.

This fact of business life holds true whether your operation is a manufacturing plant, service organization, distributor enterprise, retail establishment, hotel or hospital. It holds true for a business that employs five people, five hundred, five thousand or hundreds of thousands worldwide. It holds true for individual working businesses and for individuals who make a business work. The blunt reality of the marketplace is that a customer is a customer is a customer. Irritate a customer—and he will grouse, grumble and desert you. Treat him like royalty—and he will beam and come back for more. And more. And more. That, in my experience, is what competition is all about.

The question is: What steps can you take to convert UCE from theory to result-producing practice? Here are some of the actions and guidelines that helped me put this concept and philosophy to practical use in my three South Florida hotels and other business enterprises:

1. Don't settle for passed-along information.
2. Become an uncompromising tyrant when it's called for.
3. Make your obsession contagious.
4. Serve as an unrelenting role model.
5. Grab your customers' attention with the unexpected.
6. Cash in on your customers' self-interest.
7. Monitor the competition—then go it one better.
8. Adhere to the 10 Commandments of Competition (covered later).

Don't settle for passed-along information

When the boss minds the pot personally on a continuing basis, it tends to keep things stirred up enough so that a tasty brew is produced.

More sales and profits go down corporate drains because high-level executives and middle managers are not intimately aware of what is going on in their operations than for any other reason. They mindlessly assume that because <u>they</u> wouldn't slight or mistreat a customer, the same thing applies to their subordinates. Not so, as experience proves again and again. Consider the following examples:

DEPARTMENT STORE: A well-dressed customer in her forties approaches a clerk in the housewares department with a cash register tape in hand. "When I was in the store the other day, this $3.50 item on the tape wasn't included in the package."

The clerk replies: "You should have come back immediately. When did you say you made the purchase?"

"I think it was last Wednesday. Or maybe—"

"Well ma'am, I see the receipt was dated Tuesday. It's not our policy to—"

"I don't care what day it was. All I want is –"

"I'm sorry, I can't help you. You'll have to take it up with Customer Service."

"Forget it," the tightlipped customer replies. "If this is the kind of courtesy and respect I get in this store, I'll never shop here again." She flounces out.

HOTEL: Passing through the lobby of my Sheraton Hotel in Boca Raton, I greeted a distinguished sixtyish-looking gentleman and his wife who had just checked in.

He had come from a competitive hotel, which shall remain nameless.

"You won't believe this," he said. "They gave us a room and when we got there with the bellhop we found the maid was just starting to clean up and make the beds. She said she'd be done in a half hour. Well, we didn't feel like sitting around while she made up the room.

"The bell hop suggested that I call the desk and took off. When I called and asked for another room, the desk clerk instructed me to return to the desk with the key, but didn't even offer to send back the bellhop. By this time I was fuming. We returned with the key all right, then marched out the front door and here we are."

Whatever kind of business or industry you are in—disservice horror stories of this kind are commonplace. In most, but not all cases, if the executive in charge of the operation knew about the way employees were flagrantly slighting or mistreating customers, he or she would be even more horrified than the customers. The solution, and an essential requirement if achieving the Ultimate Competitive Edge as your goal, is to pay <u>close</u>, <u>constant</u>, <u>personal</u> attention to the way your people are handling—or mishandling—customers.

My policy and practice as a business owner was to mingle and interact with the customers of my hotels and other enterprises to the maximum degree possible, and to require my managers to do the same. No less than thirty times on the average day, I stopped customers in the lobby, hallways or restaurant and introduced myself to become personally acquainted with them.

"Hello, I'm Bob Levinson. I own this hotel. How are you getting along? Is your room okay? Are you satisfied with the service? Is there anything I can do for you?"

You can adopt this approach whether you run a hotel, plant, warehouse or retail establishment. Establish personal contact with your customers. Ask them how they like the product or service. You may be surprised by some of the answers you get.

The other side of the personal awareness coin is close and constant observation. Watch your people in their dealings with customers. Evaluate their attitude and the customer reactions they elicit. Eavesdrop on their conversations. You can do this subtly and tastefully; you shouldn't and don't have to be intrusive. Let your employees know they are always "on stage" and watch the effect it will have on their behavior. Realizing that you are OBSESSED on the subject of service, they will understand and respect your concern.

Become an uncompromising tyrant when it's called for

In the final analysis, competition boils down to your salespeople versus your competitors' salespeople and your customer contact employees versus employees in competitive enterprises who interact with their customers. If you could transfer all the ineffective and attitudinally-deficient people on your payroll to your competitors, you would wind up king of the marketing hill.

Unfortunately, that isn't realistic. Even if you could affect the transfer, it would not necessarily result in achieving the Ultimate Competitive Edge of Superior Customer Service, because employees who give second-rate service aren't born that way or inherited—they are made. They are developed and nurtured by a combination of managerial neglect and supervisory indifference. I find it hard to believe that with so many commercial, industrial and retail customers victimized by inferior service, there is still so little being done about it.

Review your operation objectively. If a customer registers dissatisfaction with his or her treatment or service, what corrective action do you take? Do you treat the complaint as a transaction where an adjustment may be necessary? Or do you dig down deeper to the people involved—those who, more often than not, are at the root of the problem? In most cases I've seen the mindless, mechanical, transactional approach is taken, and it rarely works.

In my experience, attending to the paperwork and ignoring the people-work is superficial. Even if the transactional problem is resolved, unless you pinpoint and correct the human reason behind the error or omission, it will occur again and again.

There are four possible causes behind every customer complaint:

1. Customer error or misunderstanding.
2. Human error by a conscientious and well-intentioned employee.
3. Human error caused by lack of knowledge or training.
4. Human error by an uncaring and indifferent employee.

An executive's attitude towards customer complaints can make all the difference in achieving and sharpening the Ultimate Competitive Edge. I view a customer complaint as a business opportunity. The way you respond can make a customer a friend or enemy. It can convince the customer he or she is critically important to you and your business or not. It can cause the customer to conclude that you run a high-quality operation or a second-rate enterprise.

Any display of customer satisfaction, right or wrong, valid or unjustified, calls for swift and thorough investigation and analysis. Whatever the evaluation, response should be immediate. If ...

... the customer is mistaken, explain the error or misunderstanding as courteously and tactfully as possible, with embarrassment to the customer minimized.

... the problem was triggered by well-intentioned human error, double-check your controls in an effort to prevent a recurrence if you can.

... the dissatisfaction was the result of inadequate employee knowledge or training, qualify the person in question, or avoid placing him or her in situations where his or her inadequacy can create a similar problem.

... the customer dissatisfaction was created by an employee with a negative and uncaring attitude, reinforce the seriousness and importance of your personal OBSESSION about service by imposing the harshest and most uncompromising discipline possible. Give him or her one chance to reform if you must, but certainly no more than that. If you settle for second-rate service from your employees, that's the best you will get.

Make your OBSESSION contagious

Far-fetched as it may sound, imagine an organization where all employees, from clerical people on up, are OBSESSED with the goal of providing customer service that is second-to-none. Salespeople would bend over backwards to ensure total customer satisfaction to the nth degree. Sales and clerical employees would respond to customer complaints and inquiries promptly, courteously and with genuine interest. Executives and managers would treat customer problems as their own personal problems. Can you imagine such an operation? It would run the competition into the ground and stomp them into oblivion.

A handful of super-serving companies do exist, but genuine dedication is rare. Time and again I hear horror stories from executives who receive brush-off or brusque treatment in response to product complaints, inquiries about shipments of goods, or requests for clarification regarding product pricing and use.

The solution to this problem is conceptually simple. Only one hitch exists. It requires effort and time, plus that essential ingredient OBSESSION. Years of experience tells me that the Ultimate Competitive Edge is achievable if the man or woman in charge of the department, division or company is *determined* to achieve it—and follows up that determination with *action*.

What kind of action? Action designed to communicate through osmosis, personal exposure and relentless repetition of the service objective and message to every sales, office and plant employee of the company. OBSESSION with service is a communicable bottom line-boosting addiction. It is contagious. Encourage and motivate your people to catch it.

Serve as an unrelenting role model

Students of human behavior agree that followers tend to emulate leaders. Line employees reflect the image and conduct of their managers. Assistants pattern their actions and responses after those of the boss. Executives, therefore, through their standards and operating style, determine and dictate the way their subordinates act and react.

This mirror effect can serve as a powerful motivational tool in striving for the Ultimate Competitive Edge. Server see, server do. It is no secret to any executive that he or she functions in a glass-enclosed cubicle. Even when you aren't consciously aware of it, your people follow every action you take and every commitment you make with a high-powered telescope—and they don't miss much.

Executives can role model excellence, in general, and superior service, in particular, in a variety of ways, if they emerge from behind their desk or conference room ensconcement often and visibly enough to observe and become involved in the operations they supervise.

Phil Salinger, marketing vice president of a Boston consumer products company, is apt to pop up any time of the day in the company's showroom, sales, production, billing, credit or shipping department, and he personally visits key accounts regularly. In the showroom, he checks shelves to assure they are properly stocked, that personnel are well-groomed and presentable, that general cleanliness prevails. "I'm a self-acknowledged snoop," he asserts. "Anyone who doesn't like it is free to seek employment elsewhere in a less-intrusive environment."

In the sales department, Salinger dips into sales correspondence, making revisions and suggestions where necessary. He checks billing often to make sure orders are processed on schedule, invoices are accurate and back orders not excessive. In credit, he keeps after personnel in an effort to avoid the credit processing backlogs that so commonly irritate customers. In the field, he drops in on accounts regularly to check stock on the shelves, determine that shipments arrived in time, and inquire about problems, treatment and service.

"The important point is that employees are reminded constantly that I am bugged on the subject of service, that I expect them to toe the service mark and that I accept no alibis or apologies for their failure to do so. You would be surprised at the difference this makes."

I can echo this sentiment from personal experience. I did my best to preach and practice the credo of superior service on an ongoing basis in all my businesses. I conducted lectures and meetings on the subject. I solicited suggestions on how to improve service in my hotels, restaurants and conference rooms. The message came across to my people and it got across to my customers.

A repetitive theme goes something like this: "What steps can we take to make your visit or vacation more enjoyable?" "What can we do to make your business meeting more successful and productive?" "How can we make your banquet or party more fun?"

I will concede this: From my employees' standpoint, I may seem like something of a nag at times in the persistence of my service-directed role modeling. But it works. My experience tells me it is the kind of nagging that commands respect and brings results. It brings in customers and keeps them coming back for more.

Grab your customers' attention with the unexpected

Take the hotel business: The expected—is a clean room with an ample amount of clean towels and crisp and freshly laundered linens. The unexpected to a business customer or guest—is service and consideration uniquely tailored to their personal wishes and needs. That extra touch. The special icing on the cake.

Whatever your business, the unexpected can be made to occur if you keep your eyes open and prepare for it.

CASE IN POINT: A guest in one of my hotels was a dedicated jogger. Each day at 6:30 a.m., he ran hard for an hour, and then returned to the restaurant's dining room and requested two glasses of water. This happened three days in a row. On the third day, a busboy was waiting outside for him with the water in hand when he completed his run—and offered this service for each day of his seven-day stay. To say the customer was surprised and flattered would be understating it.

CASE IN POINT: Hotel guests and business people from abroad who participated in conference or seminars rarely encountered language difficulties in obtaining information and meeting their needs because our personnel roster included employees fluent in Spanish, French, Japanese, German and other commonly spoken languages. Today, with the aid of the centralized computer system, language assistance can be quickly provided. Thus, Spanish-speaking guests, for example, anticipating a problem in making themselves understood, find to their relief that this problem is unexpectedly solved.

CASE IN POINT: Years ago, my wife, Phyllis, purchased two or three pounds of meat in a Kroger food market while at our summer home in Cincinnati. She brought home the package and put it in the refrigerator. When she opened the package a couple of days later to prepare the meat for dinner, she found it was spoiled. Returning to Kroger, she explained what happened. The meat department employee, without even asking for the sales receipt, immediately and cheerfully refunded her money and profusely apologized for the inconvenience. Needless to say, Phyllis was pleasantly surprised by treatment so rarely found. She must have told at least twenty friends and neighbors what a great store Kroger is.

CASE IN POINT: It was after 5 p.m. when an obviously upset customer telephoned Michael Dorota, owner of a small television parts manufacturing company in Passaic, New Jersey. Dorota was the only one left in the plant, but the customer had a second shift scheduled and had inadvertently run out of a part that would soon stop production cold. "No problem," Mike assured the worried plant manager. "I'll drop a couple of cartons off on my way home. You'll have them within the hour." Dorota's home happens to be in the opposite direction of the customer's plant. The customer knew that and couldn't find words to express his gratitude.

No bottom-line boosting strategy will compare with that extra dimension of service, that unexpected supplier response which takes the customer by delighted surprise. It may entail a bit of extra effort and time on occasion, and a little imagination as well, but it is the most surefire way I know to achieve the Ultimate Competitive Edge.

Cash in on your customers' self-interest

Customers, whether they patronize hotels, hospitals, retail stores, financial institutions or manufacturing companies, have one thing in common. They have highly individualized needs and objectives and they want to be made to feel that the people with whom they exchange their hard-earned money for goods, services or advice consider them to be very special and important. Customers want ...

- Suppliers who respect them and their money.
- The ego-nourishing feeling that they made a wise decision in their choice of supplier.
- Assurance and conviction that the supplier is on their team in helping to fulfill their money-making, money-saving or pleasure-getting goals, whatever they may be.

It is standard business procedure for companies that supply goods and/or services to plan hard and conscientiously to determine:

- How the product will be sold and distributed.
- The price levels and terms of sale.
- Product unit and packaging
- Repair, returns and replacement policy.

Only rarely is comparable time and thought devoted to the sales and service policy <u>from the customer's point of view.</u>

One problem I have found is that in formulating business strategy and decision, many executives tend to take a kind of detached and mechanical approach with regard to sales and service. Instead of trying to put themselves in the customer's place—for customers are the same the world over—they think of customers as dehumanized entities.

Adopt this simple perspective and it will help you immensely: Superimpose <u>yourself</u> on the selling or service situation at hand. After all, whatever business you are in, you are also a customer. Through constructive snooping and sniffing, find out how your customers are being treated in their various dealings and transactions with the company. Then ask yourself how you would feel and react if you were treated that way.

A study conducted by Technical Assistance Research Programs, Inc. (TARP) disclosed that consumers who were completely satisfied with the level of service received told an average of four to five people, while consumers who were dissatisfied told nine to ten people. In virtually every business enterprise I have ever known, word-of-mouth referral was at least as powerful a bottom line booster, if not more powerful, than any sophisticated marketing or merchandising strategy you could name.

As TARP concluded in its published report, "Companies work very hard to develop good products and services and to attract new customers. During product delivery, however, the customers' real needs are forgotten. Marketing falls in love with its own 'hype,' and operations will implement standards which are easy for them to conceptualize, measure and fulfill. Unfortunately, customers are more interested in their needs, and their unfulfilled expectations translate into lost revenue and higher after-sale costs."

Human nature is no different in business than on the home front or in the community. Catering to the personal self-interest of the people you deal with wins friends and, as an automatic byproduct, results in material compensation as well. The specific actions that yield the greatest reward are usually not listed in corporate manuals or sales policy directives. They are uniquely tailored and individualized to personal needs. For example:

- A sales rep calls a customer, unsolicited and on the spur of the moment. "Look, Jack, I was just thinking about your operation. Unless I'm mistaken you could save about six thousand dollars a year if you..."

- "Ellen, what do you think of this idea? You know that monthly product status report that we send to you that takes your department time to transcribe into useable data? Well, since you use XXX program, we could send that report to you in a way that your department wouldn't have to work with to use it."

- "Frank, I just read about a doctor who has a program of back exercises that has been written up in the medical journal as remarkably effective in relieving lower back and muscular pain. I thought your wife might be interested. Here is his address and phone number..."

All it really takes is a genuine interest and concern in the health, happiness and welfare of the people with whom you interact and do business. As any top-earning salesperson would confirm, the payoff is rewarding, not only in terms of sales volume and profit, but also, more significantly, in terms of human fulfillment as well.

Monitor the competition—then go them one better

The more you know, the faster you grow, the higher you go. In no area of business is this more applicable than with regard to competitive intelligence.

When I was with Steelcraft Manufacturing Co., where we produced a single product—metal doors and frames—and devoted every effort to achieve unsurpassed quality, we lived by a credo that worked even though our prices were high. Our overriding objective was to find whatever ways and means we could to make our customers successful in their business. In my opinion, that's what competition is all about: Contributing more to your customers' success than your competitors.

It is a two-part endeavor. Part One is the task of keeping constant tabs on what your competition is doing to ensure customer satisfaction and loyalty. Part Two is developing a program that is more attractive than the other guy's. If your chief competitor comes up with a pretty good inventory control package, you come up with a package that makes his setup seem shoddy by comparison. If your competitor announces a "deal," you develop a super-deal.

At Steelcraft, the competition was fierce. They made some products that were almost as good as ours and then chopped their prices to the bones. I can tell you, our observation posts were manned with sharp sentries equipped with high-powered telescopes focused on competitive moves and maneuvers. The challenge was to go them one better—and we made every effort to do so.

On one occasion we ran a sales meeting, not with selling strategies in mind, but with strategies designed to enhance customer profits. Five hundred customers were invited. The announced theme was: "How To Do a Better Job In Your Business." We hired experts from various fields to give our customers tips and pointers that pertained to their businesses. Prior to the meeting, we had researched some of our customers and obtained specific information regarding their special problems and needs, which was what we addressed. Everyone waited for the company pitch for our own products. But it never happened.

Admittedly, the program was expensive—but the payoff in reinforced customer loyalty was well worth the cost. When you imaginatively and constructively go out of your way to build your customer's business and make it more profitable—and monitor the competition regularly to be sure you are doing a better job toward this than they are—the boomerang effect is inevitable. As the old proverb goes, "One hand washes the other."

Adhere to the Ten Commandments of Competition

Follow these Ten Commandments religiously, and the Ultimate Competitive Edge will be an automatic byproduct of your dedication and devotion to service:

1. Make high-level service an absolute and unwavering OBSESSION. Practice super-service yourself. When you are not practicing it, preach it.
2. Maintain top- and high-level executive visibility. Whenever possible, have members of top management interact with customers.
3. Publicize owner identity. If you are an independent owner, spread the word and capitalize on it.
4. Work hand-in-hand with customer contact people. When salespeople appear with prospects and customers, meet with them, even if briefly, and voice your feelings about customer service.
5. Give key customers your personal telephone number. You will rarely be called during off-business hours, but when you are, it will be calls you wouldn't want to miss. Take a cue from top insurance industry reps: Be accessible.
6. Let as many people as possible—employees, customers, suppliers, service personnel—know you are addicted to superior customer service.

Fanaticism and extremism rarely pay; this is one notable exception.

7. Make as many personal calls as you can on as many customers as you can—to thank them for their business, if for no other reason, and to make sure they have no problems or complaints.

8. Don't screen telephone calls in general, but customer-calls in particular. The last thing you need is a buffer between you and the customer; it only serves to dilute the information you receive.

9. Seek opportunities to be of unique and special assistance to customers. Unusual service is one business surprise that delights.

10. Make new account follow-up a must. Contact new customers as quickly as possible to thank them for their business, to ensure they have no problems or complaints, and to solicit their ideas and suggestions. Get the message across to all customers that your interest in them and their importance to you will continue after the sale and for as long as you do business together.

26

ACT LIKE THE OWNER

"*B*orn *to be a man—died a grocery clerk.*" So goes the simple epitaph inscribed on a Paris tombstone. The grave's occupant, an unfortunate named Arsene, hanged himself in a fit of depression.

Makes you think, doesn't it? The desire to get ahead torments most of us to varying degrees. Rarely to the extent that it did poor Arsene, fortunately. Still, when you face up to the hard reality of the matter, there is a lot at stake. Those who stand still in life miss out on so much. Not just the things that money can buy. Much, much more. They miss the feeling of elation that comes with success. The challenge. The zest. And most of all, the supreme self-respect.

Well, Arsene is gone. We can't help *him*. But *we can help you!* Or, more accurately, we can help you to help yourself. We can help you make sure you don't wind up in the role of "grocery clerk." How?

By hammering across to you this potent savvy tip: If you want to run an important part of this show, maybe even, in time, the main part of the show, if you want eventually to become the owner of the business or stand up right there alongside him, the trick is to *ACT LIKE THE OWNER*. This savvy tip can propel you right to the top.

How do you act like the owner? You begin by *thinking like the owner*. You learn what goes on in an owner's mind.

You learn their desires and how to satisfy them. You learn by understanding what they are, what makes them tick. *By training yourself to see beyond the BENEFITS of ownership, and appreciating the PROBLEMS of ownership—and then taking positive, self-motivated action to help get them solved.*

Understanding ownership. How does it come about? Listen to this sardonic piece of advice offered by a colleague: "Be alert," he said. "Work hard, do a good job every day—and who knows? Some day you may own the company, work in a big private office, and have the privilege of worrying about staying in the black, the pleasure of meeting the payroll, and the happy task of beating competition."

The point is clear. The owner's route is anything but rose-strewn. It's tough. It's thorny. But I've yet to have one owner tell me that the road's not worth the trip. On the other hand, show them a way to smooth the path and they are eternally grateful.

"The soundest way to progress in any organization," a top business leader once said, "is to help the person ahead of you get promoted."

The person may be your boss, or your company's boss. It makes no difference. When you boil it down, it's just another way of saying:

Act like the owner!

Identify with the owner

One thing about any savvy manager: They are strictly a WE-person. *They identify with the owner.* It's not "the" company or "their" company. It's our company.

In the savvy manager's eyes, *their* company is the greatest in the world. So are its people, its progress, its products, its achievements, its goals. Savvy managers know that when they give their company a boost, they give themselves a boost at the same time. That's the WE-approach. *It's acting like the owner.*

Is this just a rah-rah talk? Or is it get-ahead talk?

Here's how one student of business answers the question: "If you work for a person, for heaven's sake work for them, speak well of them and stand by the institution they represents. If you don't," they added, "the first high wind that comes along will blow you away, and probably you will never know why."

The decision is strictly yours. Do you want to be "blown away?" Or catapulted to the top?

Firing line proof? Here's a good example. When a new Steelcraft distributor came to our plant in Cincinnati for the first time, Steve, one of our young employees, drove to the airport to meet him. An hour or so later he brought the distributor in to meet me and my brother Charles, who run the company.

Well, what can I say? It's hard to define. But from the moment the distributor entered the room, we knew that Steve had done his spade work well. We didn't have to *define* it. We could *feel* it.

It was a nameless something about the way the distributor grasped our hands. It was the look in his face, the glow in his eyes. That told us more eloquently than words that Steve had managed to spark the distributor with his own enthusiasm for his job and his company.

I don't know exactly what Steve said to that man. I don't care what he said. More important was the way he said it, the way he felt it, the way he hammered through his feeling to an individual who meant a great deal to all of us. I hope you get the point, because it's a mighty important one.

Who is Steve? Top management? Key man? Well, yes, in a way you might say Steve is a key man; at least he is as far as we were concerned. Actually, he was hardly past his teens, not a year out of school. But in our eyes, he was a key man of the utmost importance—because we knew then that he had the magic touch. Steve's savvy build-up was well started. He was on his way up and up and up. Why?

Because he acted like the owner!

Grow with the company

The fact is this. Growing with a company is a kind of unspoken mutual-agreement pact. Your part is to contribute everything you can to your company's success and to have faith that your company will keep its part of the bargain and contribute in fair measure to your success.

What does your contribution consist of? The truth is, if you want to get ahead, *really get ahead*—and I'm not talking about a token raise or a fancy title, I'm talking about the real thing, that trip to the top—you must be prepared to **SACRIFICE**. That's what your contribution consists of.

Why? Because *the owner* is prepared to sacrifice. And in order to act like an owner, you have to emulate an owner.

Sound rough? Maybe it is, depending on your point of view. Depending on what you want to *achieve* and what you're willing to *pay* to achieve it. I promised to level with you. Now I'm leveling, and if you want out, this is the time to leave. But I can tell you one thing: If you think there is any comfortable, plush-lined road to Owner-land, forget it. The road is rough and ragged. It's lined with sacrifices. But there's one overriding grand and glorious consolation—big as the sacrifices must be, the payoff is even bigger. Again, I'm not talking about money alone. I'm talking about personal satisfaction, personal gratification. "In the end," says one sage, "men love better for which they have made sacrifices than that through which they have enjoyed pleasure."

Sacrifices? What kind of sacrifices? All kinds. For example:

There was a big Miami convention, a trip our Midwest people looked forward to with relish. A week before the convention, I asked one of our managers:

"Well, Jack, all set for the trip?"

His response was a shade sour.

"Can't make it this year. I'm working on a contract I don't want to delay. Besides, I expect a guy in from Albuquerque. Been trying to close a deal with him for months."

It's just one small example, but we all knew Jack wanted to go to Miami. And he could have gone. The only thing that stopped him was himself, because it would never occur to him to permit his personal preferences to stand in the way of the company's goals.

Maybe his sacrifice wasn't exactly earth-shattering. But it's the kind of action that hits me, as an owner, where I live. Because, in Jack's position, I know I would have made the same decision.

What about you? What would you have done?

Here's another case. We had some work to give out, a profitable piece of business for someone. I knew one of our people had a close friend with the unique facilities to do the job. I asked him about it.

"What do you think? Would your friend like to handle this job for us?"

"They'd love it," our manager replied. "But there's another outfit I heard about that will give us better service for a lower price." I gave him the green light and he contacted the other outfit.

Do you get the picture? Faced with an opportunity to throw a close friend a lush job, our manager turned it down. Why? Because he acted like the owner. The company came first.

One of our managers who held down an administrative post was especially knowledgeable on the subject of fringe benefits. One day I had an idea for a new benefit for our people, so I went to this manager for his reaction.

"Do you think they'll like it?" I asked.

"They'd love it, he replied. "But it's a rough benefit to administer." He discussed some of the problems. "I think the headaches would outweigh the values. Much as I hate to say so, I would advise against it."

See where the sacrifice comes in? This man has a big family and would have profited greatly from that benefit. Still, he was instrumental in killing it because, just like an owner, he couldn't find it in his heart to recommend a move that would be bad for the company.

But there's another factor, too. And that's where the faith comes to play. These managers knew—without a word being said—exactly what was involved in the sacrifices they made. And they knew that I knew it, too and that somehow or other I would make it up to them in the end and that eventually they would wind up ahead of the game.

Don't over-socialize

Here's another kind of sacrifice, and this one separates the managers from the managed.

Example: This friend of mine held a key executive job in a company not far from our own. He had developed a very close friendship with a fellow executive and the two men and their wives became inseparable. Parties, bridge, golf, the whole bit. Very nice. Very pleasant.

Until one day things started happening in the company. Major changes. Old policies revised, product lines switched, new goals established. In the end, my friend was made executive vice president. His friend, because of product changes and other factors, was released from the company. The reasons for his release were pretty obvious. His special skills just did not fit into the new setup. A terrible scene ensued. The other fellow felt my friend could have saved his job—and maybe he could have kept him on in a non-productive capacity. But he was too fine an executive to do this. Friendship or not, his dedication to his employer and his company's goals would not permit him to do it. The windup was that the friendship erupted into the ugliest kind of enmity. It left a scar which my friend knows he will never be able to completely erase.

The conclusion is clear. It's risky for people in management positions to over-fraternize with their associates and subordinates. The vicissitudes of business are too unpredictable. All too often, what has to be done, has to be done. This, too, is a sacrifice that savvy managers must make, and sometimes it is the most difficult one of all.

Reluctantly, but realistically, what I'd recommend is this: Keep that friendship and goodwill with your associates warm and glowing. Keep that mutual feeling of respect and admiration actively alive. But take care not to extend the relationship too far beyond the confines of the job into your social and personal life.

Getting in the act

It is time to get *you* in the act. *Fact One:* Management savvy in its purest form is simply human savvy applied to business. It is doing *unto* others, instead of to them. It is what I like to refer to as *people-izing*. *Fact Two:* At some point in your career, the savvy manager wakes up to a strange and wondrous revelation. You will realize that the boss is human, just like everybody else, and that, being human, if you make sacrifices for them, they will show their gratitude by giving you the kind of boost you are after.

So get ready now to indulge in a bit of soul-searching. **Question:** How badly do you want to get ahead?

How important is it for you to wind up managing that "grocery store"—or owning the grocery store—instead of just working in it? If I've guessed your answer right, and I think I have, the next step is to put on that sacrificial cape. Sound hazardous? It's not. In fact, it won't even hurt. You may even grow to like it. Most savvy managers do.

As one philosopher said: "It is what we give up, not what we lay up, that adds to our lasting store."

So let's get that store in order.

Objective: To convince the boss that their goals are your goals, their problems your problems. **Question:** (And you're the only one who can answer it.) What action can you take—*I'm talking about sacrifices that you are not* *compelled to take*—to prove your loyalty, devotion and allegiance to the company?

Think. For some, the answer may be extra time volunteered for a project. Or extra thought given to improve an operation or solve a special problem. Or creating harmony in the shop where friction formerly existed.

Think first of the action, then how your boss would react to the action, and what it would mean to them. Ask yourself what they, as the owner or the owner's representative, would like most to achieve or unsnarl.

Now get out a pencil and pad. Jot down three or five right actions to take—as many as come to mind. Actions made as sacrifices *above and beyond the call of duty,* if you will. Then get cracking on them tomorrow, or sooner, and watch with amazement the boss' response.

Agitate for profits

Somebody once said, and they must have owned a business: "No statue was ever erected to the memory of a man or woman who thought it was best to leave well enough alone." This swings the subject back to our main theme: ACT LIKE THE OWNER.

Question: What does the owner do most of his or her working time? *Answer:* Directly or indirectly, they track down money-making and money-saving opportunities. They sharpen, they tighten, they improve. *They agitate for profits!* And they do so on their own. Nobody pushes or prods them.

Profits! Here's a tip: Bite into that word. Chew on it a while. It's the most important word in the owner's lexicon.

All right, back to the firing line. Scene I. It concerns Manager No 1. I'm an owner, so I snoop, I pry, I agitate. One day while walking through the plant, one of my favorite pastimes, I entered a department and spotted trouble at once. Things were too chaotic, too piled up. Obviously, a bottleneck. You can sense these things after a while. I scanned the floor for Manager No. 1 and found him checking a shipment. We discussed the bottleneck and tried to get to the root of it. I pointed out a few things, fired a few questions. Why this? Why that? I pushed; I prodded. Finally, I got him to act. All right, Scene I, curtain.

Now, Scene II and Manager No. 2. He runs another department. One day he came to me and called a problem to my attention. "Now here's what I think should be done about it..." He outlined a plan to solve the problem. *On his own!* Without pushing, without prodding.

Get the distinction between No. 1 and No. 2? Number One is okay; he works hard. He does his best. But, he's not *owner-oriented*. He's average, ordinary. He needs the prod. Not Number Two. This manager has savvy.

Here's another case: One of our salespeople flew out west. The day they arrived, they called to inform me that one of our distributors was planning to retire and turn the distributorship over to someone else. Now here's the point: This salesperson's mission of the moment had nothing to do with this distributor's actions. It had little direct relationship to their job. Still, they felt it was important to keep me informed. They questioned the effect on the change on our profit picture. Get the idea? They didn't have to take this initiative. They took it upon themselves to do so. They self-started. In their own way, they profit-agitated.

Start the ball rolling

There's another thing about an owner, about the way they agitate. If they are a true agitator, if they are not an ivory-tower manager, they circulate. They are here, they are there; they are everywhere. There were managers I tried to hit with this message, because somehow or other I always found them glued to their desks. "For Pete's sake," I would say to them, "if you're a manager, manage. Get around the shop. Start wheels turning; start balls rolling."

Here's what I mean.

Example: A meeting's in progress and I sit in for a while and I see that things are bogging down. All right, I'm an owner, a manager. So, I toss in a comment or two, a thought-provoking idea. I get people thinking. I whip up interest. Then, I take off. How long did I spend there? Five minutes. Maybe ten.

Example: I've got a long letter to answer, several points to cover. What do I do? I sit down for ten minutes or so, outline the main points, turn the outline over to someone on my team, who responds like a pro. Trained to complement my thinking, the person glances at the notes, asks a question or two and that's that. More wheels turning. What next?

Example: A production problem awaits a solution. I sit down with my production leader and their assistant. We discuss the problem. Or, more correctly, *they* discuss the problem. They're better qualified than I am to come up with the solution. I just steer the discussion. I start the analytical gears grinding. Once this is achieved, I disappear.

It's *you*-time again. *Destination*: Top Executive Suite. *Success Strategy:* Profit Agitation.

Step one. Get out that pencil and pad and prepare for a mental excursion to your shop. It makes no difference where you work. Factory or foundry, warehouse or office, it's all the same. One thing is common to all job situations. I'm talking about *problems*. Wherever you work, you can be sure that problems exist. And problems are costly, worrisome, irritating. They eat into profits.

So start now to make that career of yours zoom. Concentrate on your company's problems and what *you* can do to help solve them. Shift from area to area of your plant or office. As ideas come to you, jot them down. And ideas *will* come to you if you ask yourself the right questions:

What does it cost? Can we eliminate that step, this part, that form? Can we use a standard item or lower cost material? Is there a less expensive process that will do the job as well? Should we automate here; de-automate there? Should we make this part or buy it; print this form ourselves or give it out to be done? Can we combine steps, components, information? Are we buying more quality than we need?

Questions, questions and more questions. And, for each question, there's an answer. Can you come up with the answers? You most certainly can if you probe, challenge, snoop and profit agitate. *But do it NOW!*

Build yourself an owner image

Here's some simple career-building logic: If you're going to act like an owner, you may as well give the appearance of an owner. This doesn't mean you should grow a moustache, buy horn-rimmed specs or strut around as if everything in sight was your property. It does mean that your owner-oriented attitude and behavior should shine through for all and sundry, and especially the boss, to see.

Now for objective number one. How do you get that owner-oriented, profit-slanted image of yours to come booming through? Talk it up around the shop about what a big brainy hero you are? Well, in a way, yes. But, talk it up with ACTION, not words. *And never be politicking.*

Somebody once said, People may doubt what you say, but they will never doubt what you do." As true as any words spoken.

It reminds me of a ball team consisting of youngsters in their pre-teens I once coached. No match for the Cincinnati Reds, perhaps, but it was a club to be proud of. Even today, people come to me and say, "Bob, I remember that club. It was a great organization. You did an outstanding job." Now, I'll come right out and admit it. I like to believe that I'm as human as they come. I enjoy a pat on the back as much as the next fellow, maybe more than some. But I can tell you this. I didn't send any press clips to these people about that ball club. The organization—and what I helped do for the organization—spoke for itself. Not because of what I *said*. Because of what I *did*.

Subtly toot your horn

Does that mean you should keep your achievements a secret? Not at all. If you make a profit contribution, it should be called to the boss's attention. But subtly, discreetly. Not by crowing about it. Not by being pushy about it. Not by saying or implying how great you are and how small the next guy is in comparison.

How, then, will the boss come to know about your irreplaceable merits? You can help them to know in 101 subtle ways. I told you about our manager who tracked down a bottleneck, came up with a remedy and brought it to me for my okay. That's one way. Another good way is to go to the boss with an idea, a plan, a profit suggestion. This will make your image soar.

Here's another key pointer: Every owner, of necessity, is interested in the total picture. If you're going to act like the owner, you, too, should be interested in the total picture. Take one of our purchasing people who came to me and asked: "How can I find out more about the sales operation? It would help me to do a better job. And it would give me a more complete view of the business." P.S. that's *my* business they were talking about. Any wonder I was impressed by that interest?

As I've said, there are 101 ways you can build your image subtly and discreetly, but the most important way of all is action. *Profit action!* As Emerson said, "The thing done avails, and not what is said about it."

So, talk less. Do more.

Open up for rapport

How can you get your people to act like owners? One: Act like an owner yourself. Two: Treat your people in a way that will inspire them to share your business views, your problems, your hopes. In short—and we're back to that favorite of mine—*people-ize!*

That's what we tried to do at Steelcraft. We tried to establish a kind of closeness and rapport. For one thing, we were all on a first name basis—and I like to think it was more than just lip service. Our top management team stressed accessibility. Every person in our plant knew, for example, that they could walk up to me at any time and say, "Bob, here's my problem..." and I would listen to their problem, cared about their problem and tried to help. I would mention it to the department head and urge that consideration be given to the problem. At least the person knew action was being taken.

Another thing in getting your people to respond like owners—*don't expect too much*. Don't expect them to be superhuman. Don't force them to put on an act. Let me show you what I mean.

There was a special profit bonus arrangement we once tried that applied under certain conditions. I felt it wasn't working out too well, and I wanted the reaction of one of my managers. So, I approached them about it. Now, desirable or not, the manager's income was determined by this bonus; how could I expect them to be totally objective on the subject? I couldn't and didn't. So, first I outlined the problem. Then, I assured them, "Don't worry about yourself. Whatever arrangement is made, your income won't be affected." Then, we discussed the details and I found out what I wanted to find out.

Then there's the problem of imitation, or emulation, call it what you will. "We are in truth," Lord Chesterfield said, "more than half of what we are by imitation. The great point is to choose good models and to study them with care."

The trick, Mr./Ms. Manager, is for *you* to provide this good model for your people. Voluntarily or not, they're going to imitate you. Your chore is to assure that "imitation" is not preceded by the letter "L."

It is no easy road to hoe. You have to play a role. You have to hide your major weaknesses, keep them a secret.

But, whatever you do, don't try to convey the impression that you're above making mistakes. I'm talking about the kind of weaknesses that undermine your owner-image, your leader-image. If you want to get high, for example, do it in the privacy of your own home, not in the presence of associates or subordinates *in or out of the shop.* If you have a job-related fear, keep it to yourself. Same thing if you feel indecisive about an important action. Don't forget, you're the one in the driver's seat and you have to pay the price. You're expected to not lose control or show undue anxiety or indecision. If you do, the weakness will be picked up and reflected by your people in their attitudes, in their performance, in their appraisal of you.

Another thing: Getting your people to act and think like an owner takes much time, much training, much trial and error and much patience. I have one manager in particular in mind who arranged a deal to do some work for a customer for a set price of $20,000. The customer said fine, go ahead with the job. Then, the customer came in and started making changes in the materials and specs, but the manager did not notify the customer of the corresponding price increases. When the job was done, a bill was presented for $27,500. The customer was flabbergasted and refused to pay—the whole thing was pretty embarrassing. But, the point is this: In making that arrangement, the manager had done anything *but* act like an owner. An owner would never have entered an agreement of that kind without working up the necessary forms and contracts in advance, getting complete approval on extras.

Okay, so the manager acted without good judgment, without savvy, not like the owner. Does this spell utter disaster? Not at all. This is where the *boss'* savvy comes into play, their training, their patience. *The really savvy managers milk every unfortunate experience for all the asset value they can get out of it.*

So, first we reviewed the problem and I helped solve it. Next, I used the incident to ensure against haphazard contract negotiations in the future. *And all this time the manager, through exposure, was learning to act like the owner.*

Also, did you notice those three points: problem-solving, training, systems? Does it ring an old familiar bell? It should. It's just one further example of getting *multiple value from a single action.*

Roundup summary—proprietor's checklist

We discussed a number of techniques that will help you to act more like the owner and that will help you to help your people act more like the owner. Now, here they are in review.

1. Latch onto owner problems and aggressively track down solutions.
2. Always think, act and talk *our* company; never *their* company.
3. Boost your company's people, products, policies every chance you get.
4. Invest *yourself* in the company with every fibre of your being.
5. Stand ready to make owner-type sacrifices to help achieve company goals.
6. Don't over-socialize with associates and subordinates.
7. Track down money-making and money-saving ideas every chance you get. It's the owner's favorite

pastime. *Agitate for profits!* Start composing and acting on your profit agitation DO-list today.

8. Move, snoop, circulate! Shift from place to place. Don't wait for profit opportunities to come your way. Ferret them out. Get others moving, acting, thinking—then take off.

9. Boost your personal owner-image, first and foremost, with productive profit actions. When necessary, throw in a bit of tactful, subtle horn-blowing to call your achievements and actions to the boss's attention.

10. Inspire your people to emulate your ownership actions and attitude by playing the proprietor's role that is expected of you. Hide your major weaknesses. Don't tip off your fears, your feelings of indecision. And, never take action that will diminish your sense of dignity.

27

WHAT TO DO ABOUT RELATIVES ON YOUR PAYROLL

Should lazy nephew Jerry really be allowed to run the receiving department?
Why is hardworking son-in-law Marvin a problem as Vice-President?
Here is advice on avoiding personnel pitfalls.

Companies that are family-owned and family-operated, as many U.S. companies are, have certain advantages over publicly held firms. They have greater policymaking flexibility and less red tape.

At the same time, family-run companies frequently develop special problems because relatives wind up in management roles. Even a solidly-based family enterprise may find itself in a hole if it fails to handle these problems wisely.

Here, based on years of experience with my own family enterprise and exposure to scores of other such firms, is some advice on how to avoid pitfalls associated with relatives in management.

Case No. 1 - Uncle George. In one company I did business with, Uncle George ran the personnel department.

Much loved by the family, he was little loved by non-family members in the business. Uncle George was underqualified and overpaid and everyone knew it. Everyone, including his nephew, the president.

But how do you confront your own uncle and tell him you are removing him from his job? This was precisely what needed to be done. Yet, the president could not face up to the task. He kept putting it off.

The result: Repercussions all over the place. Repercussions when Uncle George hired a production manager who was even less-qualified than himself. Repercussions, when, thanks to Uncle George, the company's compensation system evolved into an unmanageable mess. Repercussions when the company got into trouble with the National Labor Relations Board over a labor practice issue. Repercussions in the form of endless battles between Uncle George and long-suffering managers.

What should be done about Uncle George? Love him. Cherish him. Even help him out financially if he needs it. But, if he must be in business, spot him where he will do a minimum of damage and where he will not be responsible for important decisions. Make him a roving goodwill ambassador, for example.

In one respect, a family enterprise is like any other kind of business. To succeed, it must be run by qualified, experienced, well-trained individuals. As far as Uncle George is concerned, the company can benefit from his good intentions and loyalty to the maximum extent possible—but at the same time, be aware and wary of his weaknesses.

Case No. 2 - Son-In-Law Marvin. Marvin was sharp, ambitious and a graduate of a good business school. When Ruthie married Marvin, the family beamed with delight.

And when his father-in-law, the president, offered Marvin the vice presidency after a one year apprenticeship, it was not true that he had gotten a job he didn't deserve. Of course, he got it sooner than he might have otherwise, but he worked hard and he was extremely competent.

Bitterness in the ranks

What, then, was the problem? As I found when I ran across this situation in a company we once considered for acquisition, the problem was disgruntlement in the ranks. Marvin's job, with its prestige and fat salary, was a plum sought after by a whole field of contenders. When Marvin won out, the inevitable conclusion was that he had been smiled upon not because of his ability, but because he had married the boss's daughter. What followed was an exodus of talented managers and seething bitterness among many who remained. One of them summed up the feelings of all: "The only way to get ahead in this outfit is to marry into the family."

Care must always be taken in promoting family members. In this case, management should have focused on two objectives: First, to get the message across that, son-in-law or not, Marvin was good for the firm. Second, management should have made it clear that you did not have to be a relative to get ahead in the company. It is important to design an attractive management development and advancement program that includes non-family members as well as those in the family.

Case No. 3 - Cousin Fred. Cousin Fred's story came to me via a company insider. Fred viewed himself as a model of the high-powered, successful entrepreneur, and he was eager for others to see him in the same light. As proprietor of a successful hardware store that he sold at a profit, Fred always made his three employees toe the line. After the sale of the store, the income from his investments provided a comfortable living.

Thus, when someone at a family get-together suggested Fred as the ideal person to head an important division of the family-owned food distributing company, several voices spoke up in agreement. If Fred's cousin who runs the company harbored reservations, he did not air them in front of the family. So, after brief and superficial consideration, Fred was invited to take over the job and he accepted.

Autocratic attitude

An overriding problem quickly surfaced. Years of uncontested autocracy as proprietor of his hardware store had turned Fred into an outdated model of the dictatorial executive. It made little difference to him that he was now running an operation employing more than 250 people and not three. To Fred, business was business and he had unshakable convictions about how a business should operate.

Example 1: A marketing idea was proposed by a veteran manager, but Fred shelved the suggestion without exploring it. Months later, a competitor came up with an almost identical strategy and made a major market gain.

Example 2: When the operation had to relocate, Fred made the unilateral decision to buy a site which gave him quick access to his favorite tennis club. The site was inconvenient for others, however, and several key people resigned.

Example 3: Thursday was Fred's fishing day; business on that day was taboo and customers be hanged. The division's fortunes started to sag soon after Fred's takeover and they continued sagging.

A different world

The first reality in this case is that running a peanut-sized enterprise like Fred's hardware store and heading up a large, departmentalized operation is like moving from sandlot baseball into major league competition. It takes a different kind of training and experience, a different philosophy of management.

The second reality is that the day is past when an executive can ride roughshod over their people and expect them to submit meekly. In most publicly operated companies, checks and balances are set up to make it difficult for one person, even the president, to take arbitrary actions that run against the consensus or are detrimental to the company. The family-held company must guard against dictatorial conduct, too.

In a nutshell, the criteria for picking a top manager is essentially the same for any profit-oriented, departmentalized organization. It is a matter of carefully screening and evaluating candidates—not on the basis of family ties, but on the merits of the candidates' capabilities.

Case No. 4 - Wife Lucy. I know a man who has two principal assets: his family-owned business and his loving wife, Lucy.

Unfortunately, the assets are in strong conflict with each other.

As can often happen in a family-owned company, the problem is that Lucy plays backseat driver from the living room sofa, dispensing advice which too often adversely influences her husband's business judgment.

To the managerial staff, she is a monkey wrench in the works.

Separate sides of life

Using a spouse or partner as a sounding board is often helpful in talking problems out, sorting alternatives, clarifying issues and weighing various factors in because a fresh, unbiased approach can serve as a vehicle for creative ideas. But, unless your spouse or partner plays an active day-to-day role in the business or has solid experience, trouble tends to erupt when they feel a need to be a part of the daily decision-making processes in the family-owned company.

What if the spouse or partner is actually part of the business? This will create no special problems, provided that they are chosen for the role based on their qualifications and treated like any other employee or manager.

Case No. 5 - Nephew Jerry. What do you do when your brother Joe takes you aside and confides he is worried about his oldest son, Jerry? To date, Jerry has been woefully unsuccessful. A dropout after one year of college, he cannot seem to hold a job. Jerry has tried his hand at five occupations and has been a washout in each.

"What Jerry needs most," Joe confides, "is responsibility, a challenge, a sense of importance. Then watch him take off."

The invitation to watch Jerry take off was tempting. A friend of mine in the sheet metal business responded to his brother's appeal by putting Nephew Jerry at the head of the receiving department, a relatively undemanding job.

Nephew Jerry is still on the job, but he is still a washout. Jerry is lazy, spoiled, unmotivated and not too brainy in the bargain. He found a home in the family-owned business. He now has a title, a respectable salary and status he could not otherwise achieve. He also has a team who do most of his work and almost all of his thinking.

Deteriorating morale

The consequence was deteriorating morale, not only in his own small operation, but also elsewhere in the company, too. During Christmas, for example, employee bonuses were cut because company orders were slow. The inevitable comment: "Get rid of Jerry and it would pay for the bonuses."

Every business is vulnerable to the ravages of the employee who does not carry his weight, but the family enterprise especially so. In business, there can be no successful compromise with capability and conscientiousness. The chances are strong that the Nephew Jerrys of this world who cannot make it in school or in the job market will flop in the family business as well.

Case No. 6 – All the uncles, aunts, cousins, etc. A talented young manager with an outstanding track record who came to work for me later confided he had turned down an attractive job offer from a competing company, also family-run.

"The word I got from my contacts," the young executive told me, "was that a non-family member in that company can advance only so far. I had no intention of getting myself into the kind of bind where I would wind up spinning my wheels."

That was unfortunate for the other company, which critically needed his capabilities.

Attracting outsiders

Hard experience has taught me that in a family-owned company it is of vital importance to make employment attractive to talented outsiders. The ideal way to accomplish this is by slotting non-members of the family into key management posts, demonstrating that opportunity is not restricted to the clan.

Failing this, the entrepreneur should be able to say honestly to a candidate: "With three brothers in top management, you may never become chief executive. But there is nothing to prevent us from one day spinning off a division and making you president of it, if your performance merits the job."

Also, of course, if you pay employees well, you will attract capable performers to your company and motivate their loyalty.

An intriguing variety of compensation plans, ranging from deferred profit sharing and pensions, to performance bonuses and health benefits, can be worked out for nonrelatives.

Stock options? In general, I am opposed to them for non-family members; the stock option too often is a poor substitute for real compensation. My basic philosophy is to provide for your people the opportunity to acquire sufficient financial resources to make the investments of their choice.

Case No. 7 - My son, the entrepreneur. I know a man of 60 who spent many years building a specialized consulting business from a struggling one-man operation into a firm employing 40 people and writing annual billings of $4 million. He decided he wanted to retire, but he also wants to pass the firm on to his sons. Therein is the problem. The younger son, who would like to step into the presidency, is not qualified to do so and never will be. The older son, who has the brains and maturity to assume intelligent leadership, has no interest in the enterprise.

So the father, who has grown weary of the burdens of running the firm and is no longer excited by the challenges, drags on, hoping that something will break. This is not likely to happen.

Flexibility and the future

It is a mistake to hog-tie a business with inflexible notions about the future of your heirs. As head of a family business, it is enough of a project for you to plan wisely for your own future.

Take advantage of the fruits of your labor in the best way you can. Live your life as you want to live it. Let others live theirs. If your child does not want to go into the business, do not press them. If they prefer to pursue a career as a musician, tightrope walker or missionary, it is their God-given right to do so. Often, the simple decision to sell the business —bringing in experts for counsel and guidance —will solve all kinds of problems for you.

One thing more: The individualism involved in family entrepreneurship sometimes is a disadvantage as well as an asset. I know one chief of a family company who stubbornly refuses to conduct business with lawyers, considering them all disreputable. Another entrepreneur equates borrowing money with sin. A third is vehemently opposed to entertaining customers in any manner.

There must be controls to prevent the destiny of an enterprise from being unalterably linked to a single individual's whims. Such controls almost invariably are present in the publicly held company. Their absence in family enterprises creates a special vulnerability.

A need for objectivity

In my experience, the best way to ensure rational, pragmatic, profit-directed decision-making in a family-oriented company is to recruit outsiders—management consultants, lawyers, accountants, industry specialists—to play an active role in the business.

It is particularly important to elect to the board of directors knowledgeable men or women who are not personal friends who will speak their minds openly. Only then will the road be paved for the uninhibited objectivity required for successful administration of the business.

What about Uncle Charley or that not-too-bright nephew? There are ways of dealing with them so as to save their pride; give due merit to their family membership without sinking the boat in the process. Uncle Charley might be transferred out of town, given a prestigious title and made to function at his level of competence where he won't hurt the company. A special department might be set up for the nephew where he will retain status, earn a reasonable income, yet be removed from the mainstream.

28

HOW TO MAKE YOUR FAMILY BUSINESS MORE PROFITABLE

No student of history will deny that the family-owned business is the backbone of the American free enterprise system. Properly operated, it can be highly profitable and help to strengthen our economy.

But along with special opportunities, unique hurdles exist not commonly found in the large, publicly owned corporation. Experience proves that if roadblocks are faced realistically, opportunities seized boldly, the payoff can be rewarding and exciting. What follows are nine hard pragmatic guidelines designed to help you make your family business more healthy and profitable.

One: Cash in on increased flexibility

At a large publicly owned, consumer-products company, a major product line was losing ground rapidly. The marketing vice president recommended that a large advertising program be launched at once to recoup share-of-market slippage. The president agreed. Both battled valiantly for the program, but after weeks of haggling it was turned down by the board of directors. Reason? So large an expenditure would not reflect well on the upcoming income statement and balance sheet. It could stir up stockholders and give investors and analysts a less than rosy picture regarding corporate profitability. The much-needed program was shelved.

Now, take the well-run family enterprise confronted by this problem. Here, the main concentration would be on what was best for the company. Red tape and delay would be eliminated. The decision maker, balancing his or her conflicting role, can make a swift no-nonsense judgment to go ahead with the program. Once made, he or she would not be beaten down. Wishful thinking? Not a bit. I've seen it happen time and again.

Such flexibility, in my experience, gives the family entrepreneur an important edge in the marketplace. They have better control over their company's profitability because they can directly increase or decrease expenditures in a hurry if need be.

Every businessperson likes to believe they have their company's long range health and improvement in mind. The family businessperson is better positioned to convert this belief into action. Where called for, they can sacrifice current earnings in the interests of long term growth. Although earnings per share is a key consideration in any enterprise, the family entrepreneur can prevent EPS from stifling their judgment and dominating their behavior. The publicly funded businessperson is not always in so enviable a position.

Two: Keep emotions outside the business

Easy counsel to give, not always easy to implement. I know one company where a foreman —I'll call him Joe — runs his department in name only. His assistant does most of the planning. Joe mainly gets in the way and is paid twice the salary he merits. But how do you fire Joe? He's been around 21 years. It's a family business, and the family knows his wife and children. So, you pretend that he's no problem.

The emotional decision is a prime hazard in the family-owned company. I have seen entrepreneurs in conflict with themselves: "Should I invest $5,000 in that new machine? Or spend it on a vacation trip for my family?" One company owner refuses to do business with an important potential customer because their families don't get along. Then, there's the feeling shared by some non-family members that they have to stay on the good side of the right family member in order to get anywhere in the company.

The solution to all this? Take aggressive action to keep emotions outside the business. Hire an external compensation expert to help set a fair and objective salary scale —for family and non-family members alike — based on job functions and skills. For example, there is no reasonable justification for automatically making the number one son president because he happens to be oldest and next in line to the throne. It will help the company avoid mindlessly established policies.

Three: Make objectivity a fetish

Some family business owners tend to be so inbred in their thinking, they fail to fuse in ideas from outside. This can be a serious mistake. Most successful family entrepreneurs I know continually seek outside viewpoints to offset internal judgments.

Evidence shows that if your business is incorporated, it makes sense to include at least one or two outsiders as directors. But, take care in whom you choose. I can recall one entrepreneur who asked their banker to serve on the board. The banker was an astute businessperson, but too close to the chief. A major problem in that company was that the entrepreneur was drawing too much salary. Because of their close ties, the banker felt it would be embarrassing to bring this up and never did. This hurt the company and, in the long run, the entrepreneur, too.

In short, when selecting directors or advisors, stay away from friends. Choose reputable business associates whose judgment you respect and whose confidence you can rely upon. What you're paying for is objectivity—and this could be hard to come by from people you know too well who might be fearful of hurting your feelings, antagonizing or embarrassing you. How much should you pay? It depends on company size and the amount of time you expect your director to devote to the business. Generally, regular meetings are advisable so that you, as the family member, will be able to take advantage of the enforced discipline of making presentations to your outside "Board."

Must your director come from inside your industry? Not necessarily. But, it is wise to select individuals who understand the kind of problems you encounter. If you're a manufacturer, pick someone who knows labor and materials. If you're a wholesaler, a businessperson who understands distribution will be in a position to serve you more intelligently. In my experience, I have found retirees are not always as effective as top managers who are currently in the mainstream of business, although there must surely be exceptions.

Management consultants, properly selected, can also add an important dimension to your business. I have found it worthwhile to bring in consultants annually, even if only on secondary assignments. Their value lies in reviewing what you have done, assessing plans and projections, helping you to true-up perspectives. A management consultant gets paid to level with you even if it hurts. Their success is directly related to the amount of help they can give you. Assuming that they are worth their salt, no one is more apt to "tell it like it is."

Four: De-personalize key business decisions

A business has a character, personality and philosophy of its own. Often this is set by a single individual, which can be a prime hazard in the family-owned company.

In the publicly owned corporation, special pressures exist on the top person to do what they ought to be doing. The family entrepreneur usually enjoys more autonomy. If, for personal reasons, they fall behind the times in such matters as marketing or technology, it can seriously hamper the company. In one family-owned enterprise, the sales manager pressed hard for conversion to a new product finish, a move several competitors already had made. The aging entrepreneur, unreceptive to change, refused to invest in the re-tooling and re-planning required. The company's growth was irrevocably damaged.

Another family entrepreneur conceived the idea of making toy tractors out of steel. They were beautiful replicas of the real thing, indestructible, designed precisely to scale. The venture, extremely successful, did not go unnoticed. Before long others produced identical models out of plastic and sold them for a fraction of the price. The entrepreneur was forced off the market although they had a winning idea because, instead of anticipating the inevitable competition and taking steps to combat it, they stood by passively while more farsighted companies took initiatives that should have been theirs.

Autonomy is not without perils. The family entrepreneur who takes Thursday off, come what may—customer or crises be hanged. The owner who considers lawyers a bunch of crooks and wouldn't hire or do business with one. One entrepreneur was unalterably opposed to entertaining customers, considering the expense against his principles. The head of one family-owned business equated borrowing money with dishonesty or worse and said, "I couldn't sleep nights if I owed someone money."

Another man I knew ran a family business successfully for more than a decade, but then he began to get lazy and bored. A tennis buff, he took off for Florida at frequent intervals whenever the spirit moved him to spend two or three weeks on the courts. Unfortunately, he was the company chief operating officer, so the business inevitably suffered from his absences. Sales sagged, share-of-market declined. In a publicly owned company, he would not have gotten away with it.

Philosophically, one might argue convincingly about being one's own man, opting for personal values and interests. But, life isn't that simple.

Managers, family or otherwise, are charged with serious responsibility. Important decisions might affect hundreds of thousands of people. I wonder if my tennis-playing acquaintance ever gave thought to the young people in his company who tied their futures to its fortunes or to the people who might be thrown out of work should his neglect result in heavy losses or bankruptcy. I wonder to what extent he thinks about the community, the suppliers and the customers who are dependent on him.

I believe that for the family business to succeed and survive, built-in controls are essential, controls which prevent linking the organization's destiny to the whims and idiosyncrasies of one person alone.

Five: Make employment attractive to non-family candidates

A bright, young financial executive seeking to make a change received job offers from two New England companies, one family-owned, the other publicly owned. He quickly decided to work for the public corporation. "With two brothers, a son-in-law, an uncle and cousins in managerial positions," he reasoned, "what chance do I have?"

The main determining factor was opportunity for personal growth. It's a point to mull over if you run a family-owned company. Smart entrepreneurs recognize the value of strategies designed to attract outstanding people. Various lures can be structured to make a career in a family-owned company appear appetizing to an outsider.

The trouble is that to many entrepreneurs, tomorrow seems a long way off. At least temporarily well-heeled, with several things going for him, the family entrepreneur may not think much about benefit programs, financial planning or future planning. But, from what I have observed, they well might. A key element of business success lies in making employment attractive to talented outsiders. Also, economic uncertainties being what they are today, they could do worse than lay the groundwork for their own long-range security.

One building block worth noting is the deferred profit-sharing plan overlooked by most family-owned companies. Here, money is accumulated in a tax-free fund, building equity continuously, which provides a secure comfortable feeling for all employees, including those who own the company.

What about bonuses? They're fine if special measures are taken to ensure that monies doled out tie in to individual efforts and accomplishments. In too many family enterprises, payouts underline favored treatment of the clan, fostering resentment and bitterness. Where guidelines and controls to guarantee equitable bonus distributions are lacking, decisions are too often based on emotions, personal prejudices, even a rough morning spent by the boss.

Employee stock plans? They don't turn me on. I have seen too many backfire. I know a manager who worked 22 years for a family-owned business. One day, he resigned for personal reasons. He had a few hundred shares of stock accumulated, but the company refused to buy it back and no amount of arguing could reverse this decision. His hands legally tied, the manager salted his stock away in a safe deposit box where it remains this day.

For a stock plan to be meaningful, provisions must be made for conversion to cash if the employee dies, retires, is fired or quits. I have seen family-owned companies draw up complex stock or benefit plans and attempt to palm them off as a substitute for a fair and decent salary. My response to such ploys is that they are rarely, if ever, worthwhile. The hood-winked employee doesn't stay hoodwinked for long. The bright would-be recruit? Chances are that he'll see through the ruse.

Six: Apply businesslike financing techniques

Success can produce failure in a family-owned business. I have seen it occur. One entrepreneur I knew many years ago mortgaged his home, invested his savings, borrowed money from friends and scraped up every nickel he could to buy a small manufacturing business for $50,000. Then, he worked his heart out to make the operation succeed and it did. Orders came piling in. The backlog grew higher and higher. Before long, he dead-ended himself. The reason: He needed another $75,000 as working capital to pyramid inventories, hire people and keep up with demand. Unable to cope with the situation, he had to sell out disadvantageously.

It's a common occurrence. Many family entrepreneurs suffer for lack of a solid cash growth plan. The fact is that any business can obtain money to operate the company if they can prove they have the ability to earn a profit. In a pinch they can turn to the Small Business Administration for help. But, many owners don't realize this. Their financial planning is nonexistent or inadequate.

A business with profit potential can get money in a number of ways. For one, it can factor receivables. Many businesses spurn this alternative because of the high cost. But, cost is only relevant to prospective earnings. Sometimes it makes sense to pay high interest rates if it is the only way to buy growth.

In my experience, most family entrepreneurs don't know how to ask for money. The most obvious move is to chart a financial course with your banker, but many don't do it. They fail to work up a presentation with the following factors spelled out:

- Current figures and conditions of the company.

- Projection of company plans for the next year or two.
- Some market background and the company plans within that market.
- How the company plans to repay the money it is asking for.

A simple, pragmatic financing plan will ensure the growth of your enterprise. It could even ensure survival.

Seven: Personalize your approach

Savvy entrepreneurs can cash in on a strategy that is easier to exercise and control in a family enterprise than in a publicly owned corporation—they can more readily and more effectively apply the personal touch. Everyone— customer, supplier, employee, community official—likes to transact business with "the owner." For one thing, they are in a position to offer the best deal and make a positive commitment. For another, there's the ego satisfaction of doing business with Number One.

I knew an outstandingly successful entrepreneur in the lighting fixture business. When special problems arose, propositions were made, requests or inquiries were received, his practice was to delegate the details to one manager or another. But, wherever possible, he stepped in himself to apply the personal touch. In some cases, he would personally finalize the transaction his team arranged or he would relay information after his team made the search inquiries or he would follow up on transactions to make sure the other party was satisfied.

His personal attention paid off. It was remembered and appreciated. Some entrepreneurs wrongly believe personal attention means doing everything yourself. It does not.

The trick is to apply the personal touch selectively where it will count the most and to delegate time-consuming legwork and details. If entrepreneurs keep themselves visible and available, they will have the necessary mobility to use their time most effectively.

Eight: Put family roles in perspective

I recently witnessed the demise of a small, very successful family-owned manufacturing business because the wives of the two principal owners could not get along.

Although they were not assigned direct roles in the business, the family business was comfortably settled and the wives of the two brothers were constantly in and out of the plant and were aware of what was going on. When problems arose, they quickly became involved in them, advising their husbands what to do and what not to do. The system worked for a while, but not for long. One wife thought her husband worked too hard, that his brother took advantage of him. The other wife thought her husband was "the brain," that his brother was holding him back. Petty jealousies and resentment cropped up. In time, a blow-up occurred and the business was dissolved.

Every businessperson can benefit from a good confidante or sounding board, an individual he can trust to bounce off ideas and decisions, but from my own experience, I find it useful to generalize. I have family members who are interested and attentive listeners; they ask penetrating questions. But, I don't turn to them for solutions to problems about which they are not deeply and intimately knowledgeable or that might affect their personal relationships with company members, family or non-family alike.

If your family member is in the business with you, your best bet is to treat them as you would any other manager or employee, according to the position they occupy. The objective, in short, is to keep the relationship free from emotions.

Nine: Make hereafter plans for your business

I know a family entrepreneur who built a shoestring operation into a flourishing business employing 200 people. By his mid-fifties, he had all the money he needed. After that, he worked only for his sons, to leave them a business as large and profitable as he could make it. When he died, he left the company to his sons with the older one in charge. Problems developed. The older son was less than enthusiastic about the business. The younger brother was jealous and resentful. Their wives and sons got involved. There were all kinds of hang-ups. What evolved was a mess.

Another father was less emotional and wiser. He willed his stock to his widow and in trust for his minor son. But the arrangements were flexible. The trustee was instructed to permit his son to take over the business if he wished to when he became of age or, if he wasn't interested, to sell the stock.

Who can say with certainty what the future will bring?

One child is gung-ho about the business. Another couldn't care less. A third child might take over the helm, but only so as not to hurt the father.

Motivations change as time passes. A person works hard all their life, but as they grow older they opt for tennis, travel and relaxation. Their counterpart thrives on the challenge and excitement of business, never wants to slow down. Entrepreneur number three, super-charged with energy, suffers a heart attack and their personal values and goals change completely.

One never knows.

The point? Make hereafter plans for your business with all of the contingencies in mind. Don't hogtie your enterprise to inflexible notions and goals. Shoot for maximum objectivity. Don't second-guess your relatives and heirs.

It is often wiser to sell the business when you wish to step down personally and divide the money equitably among family members and principals. If you decide to perpetuate it, be sure your desire for perpetuity is shared by those individuals who will constitute the management team. Finally, if you do decide to sell, bring in experts to help you make a proper appraisal and lend objectivity to your thinking process.

The family owner's four dominant roles

1. Stockholder. Like any shareholder, they are concerned about earnings per share, getting the largest return on investment, the long range security of his holdings.

2. Manager. As a manager, their prime responsibility is to their people and ensuring their company's long term expansion and growth. Their main goal is sustained profitability, increasing sales volume and their company's share of the market. Unlike

the public manager, their tendency is to hold back dividends to conserve cash for operations and expansion.

3. Entrepreneur. Their entrepreneurial sights are focused mainly on the future, on diversification and expansion. Regardless of profitability, they insist on good cash flow.

4. Employee. Like any other employee, they are concerned with the income they can get from the business on a current and long range basis. They think hard about the future well-being of their immediate family. They want long term security and benefits designed to protect them should disaster or adversity strike.

This variety of sometimes conflicting roles exists to some degree in the publicly owned corporation, but is far more pronounced in the family business. Properly understood and pulled into perspective, it can, as we shall see, be sagaciously turned to the entrepreneur's advantage.

29

HOW TO MAKE YOUR FIRST BIG CHANCE COUNT FOR MORE

How would you like to climb the corporate ladder two or three rungs at a time? How can the young would-be manager rapidly climb the ladder to success?

The way you act on your first job will make you a "comer" or a "status-quo" type. To help you move up fast, plan future goals, sell your ideas, keep communications succinct, use your time optimally, keep your initiative alive and develop other valuable skills.

Studies prove that the way a young would-be manager acts and reacts on their first job will, in large measure, determine how fast they will climb and where they will wind up five, ten or even 15 years from today. Your first job will set your rate of growth. It will serve to call top management's attention to you as a comer if you have what it takes. Or it will classify you as a status-quo type if you wait for the breaks instead of taking positive action to make them occur.

How can you make your first big chance count for more? My experience as chief executive of a fast-growing manufacturing company and vice-president of a corporation well up on Fortune's 500 list has taught me that the surefire way to scramble up that ladder is, first, to work with and through people to accomplish your predefined goals and, second, to manage your time in a way that will permit you to concentrate on training and developing your subordinates' capabilities to get the job done right. This will free you from the operational hassles and details that tend to bog down most managers.

The following are get-ahead guidelines to reach your goal fast:

Guideline No. 1: Make a years-ahead progress plan

A career is an endless succession of goals. You are given an assignment to fulfill. You do it well and get another assignment. The process repeats itself again and again. As you keep on doing well, the assignments grow more and more challenging. The more challenging they get, the more valuable and high-priced you become. The faster you grow, the higher you climb.

This process rarely happens by chance. Most growth is planned growth. You set a goal for yourself and you work toward that goal. You establish goals for next year and for years beyond that. You study, inquire and read with a set goal in mind. You develop contacts and business associations with a set goal in mind. You sell yourself, your capabilities and your ideas with a set goal in mind.

In my experience, the best way to climb the corporate ladder is to become the person everyone comes to when the going gets tough. It is the inside consultant who is respected most in their company. Their name comes up in key conversations —including the ones that deal with promotion.

How can you become your company's resident expert on just about everything, and, as a consequence, climb and keep climbing? The trick is to identify your personal strong and weak points as they relate to your present job, the job you're currently shooting for and, when that is achieved, even the job after that. Knowing this information will help guide you in preparing, studying and eventually qualifying as the resident expert.

Guideline No. 2: Sell your ideas and make your ideas sell you

Napoleon Hill, a man who made it to the top, once told a reporter that "ideas are the beginning points of all fortunes." Well, here's news: They are also the launching pads for successful careers.

Here are some questions, and evidence proves that the way you answer them will have an important impact on your future:

- How effectively do you apply your imagination to the various aspects of your job?
- Once you generate an idea, how well do you sell it?
- How effectively do you respond to the ideas generated by others—your peers and your subordinates?

I knew a brilliant young manager. Ex-manager. He tackled operating road-blocks with relish and worked out clever solutions to complex and difficult problems. After six months on the job, he had established a reputation for himself as a first-rate idea man. What's more, when it came to selling his ideas, he was glib and persuasive. Still, his career progress bogged down.

The reason: He tripped over his ego. Where his own idea was involved, he'd embark on a selling and action crusade with unbounded gusto and energy. Unfortunately, he couldn't see past his conceit. When the idea was somebody else's, he quickly lost interest and it showed. If a subordinate came to him with a suggestion, he was usually impatient and bored.

Failure is inevitable for this type of leader. The me-oriented manager, however brilliant and talented, still needs the support of his superiors, peers and subordinates to advance up the ladder. When an idea is born, conceived by you *or by one of your people*, it is a blessed event and should be treated as such.

Examine every idea that crosses your desk. If it has merit, take every action you can to keep it alive and to encourage the originator who presented it to produce more of the same. Savvy managers manage ideas received from all sources just as well as they manage the operations, transactions and people. Sell ideas well, and they'll sell you in the process.

If a team member down the line in your department comes up with a brainstorm, that idea is their baby. If they weren't proud of their offspring, they wouldn't have shown it to you in the first place. If you scorn or ignore their creation, you strike them hard where it hurts the most. It is no way to win friends.

How you handle a suggestion that couldn't possibly work will determine whether that person will bring you their next, and possibly spot-on, suggestion. Even if you see the suggestion's weaknesses at once, let them know that you appreciate their efforts and will give it some thought. They will leave with a smile—the boss is considering their idea. The next day, sit down with them and, after thanking them again for their effort and inviting more of the same, discuss the flaws in the suggestion and help them reach the same conclusion on their own. You can squelch the idea without squelching the employee. Get the message?

Guideline No. 3: Keep it simple, keep it clear

From what I have seen in business, more goals get bogged down by fuzziness and uncertainty than by any other reason. The underlying cause is usually people who are underdeveloped, under-motivated or lack the guts to face an issue squarely. The person could be the managerial hopeful directly, or, just as bad, one or more of their subordinates.

In my experience, the young men and women who advance most rapidly in their companies are the ones who focus most effectively on action-geared communication in their dealings with others. According to the experts who make such studies, 70 percent of the typical manger's time is spent communicating. The higher you climb, the more communicating you will do.

Whether the message you're to hammer across is written or oral, the faster you get to the point, the quicker you let people know what you want done or approved—and the more time you will save.

How can you translate your thoughts swiftly and efficiently into profit-geared action? Get to the heart of the matter with as little preliminary hogwash as possible. A simple solution to keeping all communications clear and concise is to require that the main theme is summed up in a sentence or two at the start, and the action necessary appears at the bottom with the specific steps spelled out. This disciplines the communicator to keep their thoughts on the beam, sets the stage for fulfilling the memo's purpose without delay, and no time is killed trying to fathom its intent.

When I asked a young marketing trainee fresh out of college how a project was coming along, I heard a long oral report of the progress, the difficulties encountered and the steps being taken to overcome them. I stopped the trainee and said, "Let's get to the point," whereupon I heard a neat summation of the situation in two minutes, gave my "good work" go-ahead and that was the end of it.

Guideline No. 4: Make your time count for more

When a businessperson hears the term "profit squeeze," the thought of the cost-price press most companies are feeling today comes to mind. But there's another kind of profit squeeze, a more positive kind —the profit squeeze that wrings increased productivity out of every working day.

Making your time count for more doesn't mean overworking or working too long. It means using your head before using your hands, and using your time imaginatively and productively.

My suggestion is to become a "clock watcher" in the positive sense of the word. Allocate time for "must-do" functions only. Plan every working day in advance and rigidly stick to your plan. Eliminate nonessential tasks. Give every piece of paper that crosses your desk the "vitality test." If you can live without it, toss it. Delegate as much as you can to subordinates to free yourself for higher-level tasks. Stay alert to pinpoint and plug time-waste leaks that can occur, from talking time to death to responding to complaints instead of fixing them so that they do not reoccur.

It's easy to monitor your operation for effective time use and efficiency if you state expected results before assigning each job and if you compare actual against expected results when the job is completed.

Guideline No. 5: Keep your initiative alive

The chief difference between the climber and crawler is initiative—those who possess it will advance; those who lack it will stand still.

Victor Hugo once defined initiative as "doing the right thing without being told." Any time a project, problem or decision confronts you, you have two options to choose from: You can be a self-starter or you can wait for a push. Only self-starters make it to the top. Waiters usually spend most of their lives waiting.

What makes one person start on his own, the next person dawdle and hesitate? Again, the key element is training. The biggest single stumbling block to initiative is confusion and uncertainty. The more you know, the more quickly you'll go —and grow. The more your people are taught, the less they will depend on you, freeing you for bigger and better things. It's when you're not sure that you stall and delay.

Another stumbling block is being afraid to put your neck out. Fear of rejection is an initiative crippler. My attitude here is no different from that of most other chief executives: I hold in much higher regard the person who attempts to take off on his own, even if he sometimes stumbles and falls, than the individual who plays it safe every time.

How can you increase your IQ (Initiative Quotient) and become a self-starter? Be aggressive, but that doesn't mean be pushy. Simply start your own motor. Don't rely on the boss to turn on the ignition. If you want to start on your own but don't know how—find out where your knowledge is lacking, then take positive action to fill the gap. Identify roadblocks in your own operation and attack each one with enthusiasm. Motivate your people to adopt the same attitude, and then provide the incentive required to do it.

Guideline No. 6: Learn to respond to emergencies

Anyone can handle a small boat when the water is peaceful and calm. It's when the waves become choppy and turbulent that a real skipper is needed. When the Pentagon contacted my company to provide special, critically-needed parts in exactly six days that would ordinarily take three weeks or more, our top executive team huddled. Then we rallied every manager, supervisor and production and office employee in the plant to the task on a round-the-clock schedule. Everyone pitched in, worked, planned and devised shortcuts to get the job done. And we did it. If there's one thing I can tell you, it's this: that challenge —that near-impossible goal, if you will —separated the climbers and comers from the resters and waiters as no other test could have done.

What it more or less boils down to is that a manager's job is to manage. And part of the definition of "manage" is handling problems by responding to emergencies with a true skipper's skill, or better yet, heading them off altogether. When the going gets choppy, the real talent emerges.

In my opinion, the expert manager is an expert troubleshooter. When trouble signs appear, the manager is much better off probing and prying, digging down deep and asking, "What's wrong?" —and then doing it before the boss gets around to that question. The expert manager recognizes that every problem they tackle and solve will add to their store of knowledge, increasing their value and skill.

Guideline No. 7: Surround yourself with winners

If your immediate goal is an important management job and your next goal is a top management job, the most critical point to remember is *surround yourself with winners —with key subordinates who won't fumble the ball when* you *pass it to them.* Put yourself on the hiring line, and after hiring winners, develop them.

I knew a manager in his early thirties who climbed from a line supervisor's job clear up to a vice-presidency in his company in less than a decade, quadrupling his earnings. However, if you had spent 30 minutes with the guy, as I had on two occasions, you would have walked away wondering, "How did he ever make it to such a high post in his company?" The truth of the matter was that he was quite unimpressive —neither dynamic appearing nor bright. In fact, the impression I got was that he was quite dull.

One day a mutual business acquaintance and I were discussing him. The other fellow knew him better than I, so I asked, "What's the secret of his success? Who does he know?"

My friend laughed. "I know just what you mean," he replied. "He's pretty uninspiring at best. But did you ever deal with his people? He's got a crackerjack team working for him. Dependable. Knowledgeable. Sharp.

And he apparently treats and trains them well. They're very good and they make him look good. His department's performance is the best in the company."

It makes sense when you think about it. The most successful managers I know, the men and women who continue to climb, are all effective compounders. They have mastered one of the most important secrets in the book:

To function efficiently as a smooth-running, profit-minded team, the people you select and develop must achieve a common understanding and acceptance to establish an agreeable blend. I call this "chemical response-ability." As a savvy manager with your sights pointed high, you cannot do your compounding too carefully.

30

THE HIGH COST OF REMOTE CONTROL MANAGEMENT

Many centrally managed corporations abound with executives who play power games at their companies' expense. Worse, argue their critics, they rob middle and regional managers of the fun —and, hence, the motivation —of managing.

It would take a special edition of *Standard & Poor's* to list all of the enterprises that, successful prior to acquisition by large corporations, tottered or crumbled after the takeover. Most big corporations acquire companies because their financial and technical experts assess them as sound operations with good growth potential. And, it stands to reason that it took a strong and sensible management to build that company to the point where it looked good to the evaluators. So, if you buy a company you think is good, one of your major goals would be taking action —or more precisely, refraining from action —to *keep* it producing profitably.

The trouble is that ego tends to rear its ugly head. Call it Levinson's First Law if you will.

The way it works is simple. The executive on the 73rd floor ("Club 73"), the lushly carpeted part, is usually pretty important if they have the power and authority to rule on an acquisition under consideration and say, "I like it, buy it." Less powerful, but also pretty high up, is the group vice-president with the mandate to control and oversee the new operation. We can assume that just as no head of a nation gets up that high in the stratosphere without a mighty ego, neither could any corporate No. 1 or No. 2 executive.

Now, the nature of an egoist is that they feel they know more than the next person, so whatever the next person can do, they can do better. So, you run into the situation where the following procedure takes place, proving Levinson's infallible First Law:

- A technical, financial and special industry analysis is made of the Toledo Toothpick Manufacturing Co. (TTM) with a possible eye to acquisition.
- The "experts" come in with a glowing report: good strong management, excellent quality control, good cash flow, fine reputation in the field.
- Corporate management negotiates with Toledo's chief executive. Both parties are amendable. The principals hit it off. Everyone believes that one and one are going to add up to five—and the deal is made.
- Now that they own TTM, the corporate steering committee and the newly appointed group vice-president sit down to study the situation in-depth, and that's where the trouble starts. They look at TTM's marketing program and find it sadly lacking. They send an industrial engineering team around to assess its plant operation and come up with the finding that it's getting only 53.765 percent productivity. They bring in technical

consultants who mike up the toothpicks and find the dimensions all wrong and the wood too hard. Accounts receivables don't come in fast enough; accounts payable are shelled out too fast.

- The decision is made to "restructure" the newly acquired company. That's a synonym for "tinker."

An executive can tinker within the confines of his own department, division or company. Or he can tinker on a remote-control basis. Hundreds of large U.S. corporations have mushroomed into multi-industry, multi-division, multi-locational structures. Close personal relationships between high-level executives in corporate headquarters and division heads in Biloxi, Frog's Gulch or Weehawken rarely exist, so it's no wonder faith and trust are missing. To establish control, profit centers are set up and strategic-planning units developed with layers of management formed in the towers to keep tight rein on the octopal arms. These managers run a fast track where the scoreboard registers winners and losers in the language of numbers.

The only way to juggle numbers is to tinker with them. And, tinkering is as natural to centralized corporate management as betting is to the gambler.

Theoretically, and, in some cases, practically, getting acquired by a big rich company is supposed to put an end to scrimping and scrounging for funds needed to finance worthwhile programs and projects. In one company I know of, a line of medical analyzers and pumps introduced the year before showed particular promise. The general manager, the manufacturing vice-president and the production manager worked together for weeks to come up with a viable, realistic and practical expansion plan that would require a near-term expenditure of $250,000. A three-page report summarizing the highlights of the plan was submitted to the corporate controller at headquarters. In response, a meeting was called that tied up division executives at the Cleveland main office for almost three days.

Scores of questions were fired at the general manager and his people by the controller and his budgeting experts. In the end, the plan was turned down pending the submission of more information "critically needed to evaluate the proposal."

"In pre-acquisition days," the general manager remarked bitterly, "we'd apply to the bank for a loan. The bankers, who didn't know us from Adam, required only a fraction of the data we'd been ordered to supply. And we were never turned down."

Motivating the troops

Another ego trip that "Club 73" executives too often take is their conviction that as managers of The Corporation headquartered in The Big City, they know more about motivating employees than those hicks out in the boondocks—despite the fact that the hicks have been running a successful operation for years, and that the hick executives have been working with, and living with, their key people for years. The likelihood that a Club 73er is better qualified or equipped to handle and motivate these people than the executive on the scene, who knows them not merely as functions and number producers, but as *people*, is slim indeed.

Management consultant Peter Drucker echoes this contention. He says: "What we really need is for a company to see that one of its undermanaged, underexploited activities is really big enough to run itself, and then spin it off as an independent business. I could name 75 places where a business with volume ranging from $50 million to $300 million could be created if the big companies could divest and get out. I'm convinced that we'll have to come to that."

A nation of tinkerers

We are philosophically and organizationally geared to produce a nation of tinkerers. Consider the following factors:

Academic grounding. American business schools train students to tinker by stressing mathematical and computer-based skills, rather than the everyday problems of making the product, meeting the payroll, motivating employees and keeping customers satisfied. The numbers-oriented MBAs end up in headquarters suites, the real managers in division factories and offices. The problems start when the MBAs interfere in the operational decisions of the division people.

Guidelines and manuals. Tinkering by the book is standard procedure in most large corporations. One major difference between the centralized and the decentralized organization is that for a great many functions and activities—hiring, pensions, labor relations, compensation, purchasing and so on—the centralized corporation publishes one book that applies for all divisions, whereas the decentralized corporation permits each division to tailor its own set of guidelines and policy statements to its individual needs. When a company is taken over by a centralized parent, the standardized guidelines invariably conflict with existing rules and procedures. It would be impossible to estimate the amount of friction and frustration this creates in the division, not to mention the waste of money and time.

Fiefdoms. A corporate fiefdom, once created and rooted, can be harder to break down than a politically-inspired government agency. For example, in a centralized conglomerate it's not unusual for a corporate marketing vice-president to have a staff of 50 or 60 people reporting to him—research people, mathematicians, economists, computer experts, statisticians and support personnel. Each one of these bodies must be justified, along with each study, survey and program initiated. More often the end result of each study, survey and program is tinkering.

Risk-free management?

Risk-free management doesn't exist. Every management decision you make is a gamble. It may work; it may not. If you hit pay-dirt 50 percent of the time, you're probably doing all right. If you hit 60 percent or more, you're riding high on the hog.

The numbers people, from what I have seen, are trying to perform an impossible feat; they're trying to take the risk out of management. They're using computer printouts to pragmatize and rationalize management decisions. Theoretically, they are often successful. Practically, it can't be done.

Theoretically, you can quantify a bunch of computer inputs and outputs, formularize a marketing or financial strategy, and mathematically make A plus B equal C. Practically, it usually doesn't work out, because you can't quantify a customer's emotional response when a delivery doesn't get there on time or a manager's gut feeling that gilt-edged curtain rods won't sell in Vermont or a sales rep's bitterness when he's transferred against his will to Blissful Creek, Mississippi. You can't quantify the human factor. You can't calculate or formularize the human factor out of existence. And, you can't take the risk out of business.

When I was at American Standard, I paid a call on Sears, Roebuck and Co., and was told that they were ready to buy $1 million worth of doors if we were interested. My contact at Sears assured me that the company wanted very much to do business with us. Needless to say, the sales department at Steelcraft was excited. They couldn't wait for me to return with the contract.

When I returned to Sears, the contract was quickly prepared. All that remained, I was told, was the formality of signing the chain's standard purchase agreement. Following corporate procedure, I submitted this to American Standard's legal department.

"Unh-uh," I was told, "No way! We can't sign this contract."

"Why not?"

"It says here that if anyone ever gets hit by a door, a liability would result and that Sears would be absolved from the liability; the liability would be American Standard's. Sorry, Levinson, no deal."

I went back to Sears and they were devastated. They really wanted those doors. But they were equally locked into a corporate rule book as American Standard was, so they had no way to bypass that ironclad clause. They suggested that their legal department get together with our legal department. That was done. Still no contract.

Now, what's the chance of anyone getting hit by a door or having a door dropped on their head? They weren't even swinging doors. It's conceivable, of course. A careless person can walk into a door; they could catch a foot in a door. Accidents happen and lawsuits can result. But to what extent do you go to avoid liability? How fool-proof can it be to do business?

I went to the president of American Standard. We talked about it and decided that the possibility of being sued by someone who was hurt by a door was a business risk and that it was a gamble worth taking. He over-rode the legal department and let me make the decision. I took the order and everybody was happy, even the legal department, because the buck had been passed.

However, I couldn't help wondering: How many good deals are thwarted, how many creative plans are stymied, how much profit is washed down the drain, how many managers are frustrated and driven to seek other jobs— all because of tinkerers trying to play it so safe that they block growth and progress instead? It's a thought to take with you.

Bad effects of pressure

Psychologists and sociologists who study such things tell us that by nature, inherently, most people are honest. But push a person against a wall to the point where his job is in jeopardy, where there's a threat that his mortgage won't be met, or that he may have to pull a son out of college because he can't pay the tuition and there is no telling how he'll react.

Wall-pushing is a favorite pastime in the school of remote-control management. Like the "Domino Theory," the process moves right down the line starting on the 73rd floor, filtering down to the 72nd, and all the way out to the boondocks. The farther down the line it goes, the more routine and mechanical wall-pushing becomes because the more depersonalized it becomes. The Top Domino is wall-pushed by the stockholders and board if, as so often occurs, they happen to have a heavy foot on the pedal called PERFORMANCE. The Number 2 Domino is tougher than rail spikes and has a hungry eye on the top spot. It's not too hard to pass the profit message along down to the 72nd floor. From there it is carried along to the divisions, bridging the gap between operations and staff, and inevitably reaching the manager responsible for cutting costs on production, boosting sales volume and squeezing better productivity out of workers.

Whatever syrupy words and inspirational hip-hoorays the message may include, two unspoken words are often implicit: "OR ELSE!" These are words, directly or indirectly intimidated, that change honest people into crooks, individuals who seek a fair and honorable place in the sun into people who fudge and cheat in the shade. More often than not, they fudge and cheat, not because they are greedy, although this is sometimes the case, but because, forced up against that hard cold wall, they are fighting for their lives.

Here is just one of many cases I've come across: A supermarket manager was pushed for a profit yield which he knew wasn't there. He knew something else, too, from the visiting delegate's ultimatum: If he didn't make the figures specified, he wouldn't be there either. He made them. He marked up selected prices outrageously and illegally; he taught cashiers how to cheat at the registers; he fudged the figures like a blind juggler. The only thing he bought was time, which was the best he could hope for —time to shop around for a new job, preferably in a new industry as well. He found what he wanted eight months later, left the store in a hopeless mess that took half a year to clean up and left personnel who had, by then, acquired sophisticated expertise in how to cheat—not only the customers, but management as well.

Sad legends of this kind go on and on and on. We have seen a growing number of indictments in recent years: such as in the American Can Company (Sam Goody) case, where two executives were charged with selling counterfeit recordings and returning fake copies for refund to legitimate suppliers; when division managers of H. J. Heinz Co. falsified accounts to show the profit they were ordered to make; when a Chase Manhattan Bank bond officer was indicted for doing pretty much the same thing.

Human beings the world over act no less than human. If a person feels his head is on the block, if the survival of his job or division is at stake, he will all too often throw not only caution but also ethical standards as well to the wind.

The feeble giant

"In practically all of our activities," the chief executive complained, "we seem to suffer from the inertia resulting from our great size. It seems difficult for us to get action... there are so many people involved."

Is this familiar lament from the head of one of today's giant international multidivisional conglomerates? It well might be, but, actually, it was an introspective evaluation of the state of the corporation made by General Motors' Alfred P. Sloan, Jr., in 1925, when the company's personnel roster was a small fraction of its current payroll of about three-quarters of a million people.

Why this persistent worry and concern over size—by Alfred P. Sloan, Jr., in the 1920s, and by scores of corporate leaders today in the 1980s, six decades later? One explanation involves flexibility. Just as a human animal that is grossly overweight moves with slowness and difficulty, the oversized corporate animal's actions and responses tend toward profit-crippling lethargy. Another point against size in the unwieldy centralized corporation is management's predilection toward rational (often computerized) decision support, as opposed to human judgment and instinct.

"Uncertainty," states New York University Graduate School of Business professor Zenas Block, "is anathema to giant corporations. Once a company is securely entrenched in its markets, uncertainty gives way to control, predictability and institutionalization—priorities that its managers, products of the schools of business administration, are trained to enforce."

Innumerable tales could be told of brilliant entrepreneurs who founded, nourished and developed small enterprises and watched them prosper and grow over the years until, lo and behold, they found themselves with unmanageable monsters on their hands.

One such story involves Wang Laboratories, which had been a fair-haired favorite of the investment community from the 1950s to its peak in the 80s. While many American companies were struggling to survive, Chinese-born inventive genius An Wang's problem was how to avoid expanding his enterprise out of control.

"It's impossible to maintain efficiency with growth at this dizzying pace," a New York-based investment analyst contended about Wang. "Something has to give and probably will without a firm hand on the reins."

Something did give. Customers began to complain about service snags in Wang's word-processor and small-computer divisions. One reason for this was the company's inability to train and develop field and customer support personnel fast enough to keep up with the workload. Another reason related to the organization's centralized structure—the company's divisions were closely controlled by the parent on a functional basis. The problems were clear to most divisional managers, but they were powerless to make corrective decisions.

The big-is-beautiful business philosophy has long been a tough nut to crack. Youth and its go-go impetus are a factor, of course. In most large corporations, telling the young go-getters to slow down would be like telling a gull to stop diving for fish. "No matter how often critics urge managers to keep growth size under control," states New Jersey educator and management consultant Leonard J. Smith, "all indications point to the growth frenzy remaining an unalterable fact of business life."

Another factor is the business-school brainwashing geared to bottom-line performance today, with each day's, week's and month's performance measured against the prior period on an ongoing basis. Smith believes that managers equate size with success, whether it's a department, division or corporation.

As The Conference Board's Wilbur McFeely once stated: "A large organization really lives on momentum rather than vitality."

Unless it is radically decentralized! Radically decentralizing the corporate giant immediately converts it from a sprawling, inflexible, waste-ridden and lumbering entity to an organization composed of 10, 20 or 50 fast-moving and decisive small business entities —provided, of course, that capable divisional managers are on hand to do the job that needs to be done.

The number-one fall guy

Every fiasco in life has its fall guy—or, as can be the case, a great mass of fall guys. In the final analysis, it is the public that is victimized by centralized management remotely administered. Centralized management fuels the fires of inflation as surely as if gasoline were poured on them.

It happens in a variety of ways. One example is the standardization that is a fetish with many large corporations. Purchasing, wages, fringe benefits, employment procedures, insurance —all are standardized to the hilt.

In one corporation I know, job classifications fit into neat little slots, regardless of what industry a division is in or where it is located. Thus, a personnel manager is P-1, a credit manager is C-1, a production manager is PR-1 and so on down the line. If a divisional P-1 job calls for $50,000 a year, that's it—nationwide. Of course, there is some leeway, but not much. No attention is paid to the reality that wages in one part of the country may be 20 percent lower than the area demands. I have seen managers receive automatic raises ranging from $5,000 to $15,000 on the heels of having their companies taken over by a conglomerate.

The increase has to come from someplace, and it is inevitably generated by boosting the selling price of the goods or services. By the same token, I could cite more than one instance where an ideally suited manager was turned down for a job because, even though this perfect candidate was worth $55,000 per year, the corporate table of organization mandated $50,000.

Again, it's the public who pays if a second-rate manager is hired in place of the one who would get better efficiency and a higher productivity yield from his people.

Another reason the public is the ultimate fall guy for the large centralized corporation is that it is the nature of the "73rd floor" occupants to stifle imagination and innovation. A classic example is the book publishing business. During the past few years most of the nation's independent book publishers have been swallowed up conglomerates. What this boils down to, in essence, is that the editor's instinct and experience, developed over years of working with author's and books and observing the marketplace, are today discounted as virtually meaningless in many publishing companies. Nowadays, the final arbiter is the computer. If an editor loves a book and feels it may be a living contribution to the literature or a particular field of endeavor, the best he can hope for is an analytical run through the computer to determine its market potential. If the computer says OK, there's a chance that the book may be published. This effectively rules out new authors, except in unusual cases, and it often rules out books that are considered offbeat and no track record exists for that particular category.

A related pet aversion of the large centralized corporation is the introduction of new products. Unless the computer printout states you can capture 10 percent of the market after the first year, many companies won't lay out the investment capital needed. I know, because I've been through this mill. It will cost, say, $5 million to bring a new product from the drawing board into production and out to the market. Centralized corporate management wants this investment recouped in a hurry with a virtual guarantee that the new product will succeed. As any savvy businessperson knows, there's no such thing as a guarantee where new products are involved. The element of risk cannot be eliminated, computer printout or not. So, the new product, however useful or promising it may appear to the division manager, never gets off the ground. And again, it's the public that pays.

D. G. Soergel, writing for The Wall Street Journal, states the case succinctly enough. "A national anti-enterprises policy is forcing would-be entrepreneurs to abandon plans for thousands of enterprises. It favors business expansions over new enterprises." A key requirement of conglomerates is to recover capital costs in a hurry. "Thus," says the writer, "the older and larger a firm becomes, the more it tends to concentrate on improving its product rather than investing new ones." Improvement is beneficial, of course. It boosts efficiency and lowers costs. But it is detrimental as well. Innovation means progress, and one might argue the merits of improving products that should have been obsolete and replaced years ago.

Another factor explaining the reluctance of large corporations to introduce new products is the "creative destruction of capital" aspect, as economists refer to it. New products make old products obsolete, along with their tooling, design and existing physical inventory, and it generally takes years to make up for the loss and generate profits on the new product line. Since the centralized corporation's favorite battle cry is "Bottom Line Now!" innovation runs counter to corporate objectives, and thus is suppressed.

'But what about services?'

From the centralized perspective, big isn't only beautiful, it's a treasure chest of sophisticated expertise as well, and Mr. or Ms. Divisional Manager—it is yours for the asking. Or is it?

A question always raised when decentralization is being considered involves the rash of services usually offered by Big Daddy to the divisions. These range from marketing and pricing consultation to research and development, data processing and compensation. The worry is: "Aren't we going to miss them?" But let's look at some of the offerings more closely from a real-world point of view. Here are three case histories randomly selected from a source file of dozens.

Case 1 —Research and Development: The company in question produced a line of rope and sling products, all manufactured in compliance with OSHA standards. Acquired about three years ago, it became a division of an Illinois-based conglomerate. The unit had a compact, highly competent research staff, which had operated successfully for several years and had created many new products that had gained wide market acceptance. Enter Big Daddy on the scene with his offer of "R&D consultation and assistance." Translation: "From now on we'll make the decisions."

Almost immediately, the centralized Sure Thing Syndrome came into play. In the past, some of the division's good ideas, and its one most profitable idea, were somewhat unconventional by established industry standards. That no longer goes. Headquarters R&D staffers subject proposed ideas to "scientific evaluation," usually computer-based. And telling a computer "unconventional" is like recommending a chiropractor to your neighborhood orthopedist. The trick is to minimize risk taking, a feat I have as yet to see succeed.

Result: Inevitable hang-ups and bog downs. Central R&D, with approximately 32 divisions to service, has a continuing scheduling problem on its hands. Thus, a not surprising scenario shows divisional product researchers in a race with competitive researchers to develop a new product in response to market needs and coming up with a hoped-for winner. But, by the time the proposed winner gets reviewed, refined and approved by the headquarters experts, a competitor's new product is already on the market.

Case No. 2 —Patents and Trademarks: In the "good old days," patent and trademark problems and needs were handled by a local patent attorney in this small- to medium-size medical supplies company. The attorney knew the people, and, after years of experience with the client, understood their problems and needs.

Today, the company, now a division, must turn to Big Daddy's in-house legal department instead of the local attorney. Prior to tackling a problem, the corporate lawyers must undergo what amounts to a virtual training and orientation program. With a host of divisions to service, this program will be reenacted every time a patent problem arises.

Result: One inevitable consequence is costly delay, which wrecks development and production schedules. The home-office lawyers have their own problems to contend with; at last report they had a heavy backlog of assignments from several divisions with no light at the end of the tunnel. From the division manager's viewpoint, the "savings" are hardly impressive.

Case No. 3 —Computer Services: In this large apparel manufacturer, inventory and sales orders were centralized to one computer system. Forty-one divisions and subsidiary units were slated to be serviced by Big Daddy. The instructions were simple and straightforward enough: "Get rid of your computers and put in terminals to our system instead. You'll save a pile." The old story.

Result: Instead of saving a pile, it became a pile-up. The traffic problem and competition among the 41 units for computer time was only part of the headache that evolved. Under the old setup, when the sales manager, production manager or comptroller requested a special report or a weekly or monthly report, the data processing manager was hard-pressed to produce it. The reason: time was limited and at a premium. As a result, executives thought twice, then once again, before requisitioning reports, which worked out much better than one might imagine. Reports that were genuinely needed to make key decisions and run the business had a way of getting produced. The fringe stuff, frivolously or thoughtlessly requested, was automatically eliminated by the diligent system in place.

No more. The new rationale was: "Hey, we've got this new giant computer at our disposal. We can get all kinds of fancy reports just for the asking." And when the floodgates opened from 41 units, you can imagine the consequence. The headquarter's computer experts were poorly qualified to determine what was actually needed and what the division could just as well live without. The consequence was confusion and backlogs compounding further confusion, with the giant computer growing more massive and monstrous each day. At last count 41 programmers were employed, ironically one for each unit.

This isn't to say that all centralized corporate services are worthless, useless or inefficiently rendered. Obviously, there are values that can at times be attributed to bigness, and, just as obviously, there are well-run centralized corporations just as there are sloppily-run decentralized companies. The preceding examples and comments were admittedly exaggerated to drive home the point. But the reality cannot be denied, that in the giant centralized organization, in particular, not all the services offered actually serve.

At its frequent worst, the large centralized corporation massages undeserving egos, stifles creativity, encourages ruinous tinkering, bows to numbers management to a ridiculous degree, alienates the public and breeds sloppy services. Today, in many key U.S. industries facing growing competition from abroad, the nimbleness and flexibility that only radical decentralization can provide are more critically needed than ever.

31

THE SELLING POWER OF OBSESSION

If I ever need a mantra, it will probably be the word OBSESSION. This is closely related to the words, "customer service." I am admittedly OBSESSED with the objective of surpassing the service provided by competitors. The trick is to persuade, and sometimes virtually bludgeon, salespeople and other personnel who deal with customers to share that OBSESSION.

No Simple Trick

Lip service helps, but it's not enough. Here are three strategies to pound the message across:

1. The most effective strategy: The message is hammered through by example. The manager portrays the role model. From the glass houses in which they function, their actions and omissions, conquests and mistakes are closely observed by others. If they give customers unique and special treatment, the rest of the band will take the cue and march to the same beat.
2. Uncompromising quality of service ranks equally high in creating and sustaining the OBSESSION mindset. It is important, in general, to be liberal

and compassionate with regard to human foibles. It is appropriate to be understanding and forgiving when an error relating to shipments, schedules, purchase agreements and the like is made. But when it comes to customer service, brook no excuse for being rude, demonstrating lack of concern or ignoring the complaint of a customer. One of my salespeople once made a mistake in drawing up a contract that cost the company more than $8,000. The mistake was forgiven. A supervisor once insulted a customer who complained indignantly about the occurrence. That person was fired on the spot.

3. The third element is imagination. OBSESSION with customer service implies service "beyond the call of duty." It takes an active imagination to provide service in ways that deviate from routine service provided by competitors. In my South Florida hotels, for example, guests included business people and tourists from a variety of distant and exotic countries. In an effort to provide special service for these guests, we maintained a roster of sales and other personnel who spoke a gamut of foreign tongues, ranging from Arabic and Greek, to Japanese and Portuguese.

The Japanese edge

Japanese business people have their share of problems and make their quota of mistakes. But there is no mistaking one major reason for Japan's success in the marketplace: What many Americans might regard as superior and unusual service, the Nipponese take as a matter of course.

In training and indoctrinating your salespeople in the concept of OBSESSIVE customer service, citing the Japanese experience is an effective way to get your message across. In leading Tokyo department stores, for example, when a customer has a problem or complaint, she is ushered deferentially into the office of a high-level executive whose first step is to offer her tea. The manager then listens sympathetically to the woman's problem, and then bends over backwards to solve it. If this happened to an American shopper, she would probably pass out from shock.

In many, if not most, auto dealerships, when a customer experiences a problem with the engine or an accessory, the car is picked up by the dealer and replaced by another one on loan until the owner's car is repaired and returned. Does such service cost more? Unquestionably. But it yields tangible gains, as well, in terms of customer loyalty and appreciation, production pressures to sustain high quality in order to minimize the need for this costly service, and good rapport between sales and service people and customers.

Monitoring and follow-up

OBSESSION with unsurpassed customer service cannot be a sometime thing. It is a matter of persistent and unrelenting attention to the actions and attitudes of sales and service personnel. It is also a matter of sustaining awareness on a day-to-day and week-to-week basis.

Management cares. Their jobs and incomes depend on customer satisfaction and loyalty. Salespeople care too, but often to a lesser degree and at times other interests and pursuits conflict with the super-service requirement. I talked super-service to my staffers every chance I found, and I never let them forget my OBSESSION. I talked with customers too, checking and double-checking the level of service they received—as they perceived it—as a regular and ongoing managerial function.

If fanaticism accomplishes nothing else, it attracts attention. My strongest feeling was that without exceptional service, I would have no business and my team would have no jobs. Get this message across often enough and persuasively enough and it is likely to stick. When I spell success with a capital S—it's for Service!

32

SEVEN SURE-FIRE WEAPONS FOR TROUBLE SHOOTERS

Don't knock trouble. It's what keeps you in business and helps you grow. If you are the head of your business, you undoubtedly have trouble to thank for it—or more specifically, your ability to cope with trouble and cut it down to size.

Depending on your point of view, trouble in business can be either headaches or opportunities. In previous chapters, we talked about putting trouble to work for you and shooting down troubles, showing you that your attitude makes the difference. Now here are seven ways of operating which I have found work as weapons against trouble:

First: Get out of the ivory tower

It's like driving a car with the windshield blocked. You don't know where you're going. When trouble lumbers along, you'll get clobbered before you have time to avert it.

Get on the scene where you can watch trouble approach and can ward it off. Savvy managers stay close to the action, the transaction and the reaction. They probe, observe, question, experiment, build up experience.

Second: Prospect for clues.

In the business of troubleshooting, one objective is to spot symptoms. There's an old French proverb, "Follow the river and you will find the sea." That's how it is with tracking down troubles.

Scout around for profit leaks. Don't settle for surface appearances. Talk to your people. Question their actions, their reasoning, their motivation. Look under the rug, so to speak.

Solve a problem a day

Here's a tried and proven success tip: Resolve each day to track down at least one item that is not being handled to your complete satisfaction. What kind of things should you look for? Here are some thought starters:

1. Workers clustered around a desk, machine, water cooler.
2. An obviously ho-hum work pace.
3. Evidences of waste, careless handling of material.
4. Angry, heated telephone conversations.
5. Abundance of workers coupled with shortages of work. A vice president of a leading national manufacturer said if there isn't a need for overtime for at least five percent of the work force, there is too large a work force.
6. The same amount of overtime for each person or each department for every day and every week.
7. Bottlenecks and delays in any area.
8. Desks piled too high with backlogged paper work.

9. Continuously confused or hectic operations in any area.

10. Attitudes of your people. If you sense that one is bored with the work, another is indifferent, a third is bitter, a fourth is irritable—those are trouble signs. But you may also spot potential leaders—people who are bright, alert, conscientious, hard-working, those you can count on to back you up in your trouble-tracking crusade.

Don't trust these things to memory. Jot down the telltale signs as you spot them: loopholes in systems, misuse of machines, tools or materials. Most of all—watch for the floundering of people.

For some reason, it's always easy to spot problems in someone else's department or company. Try to visit other companies and look over their operation.

In short, play the role of the trial attorney gathering evidence.

Third: Saddle key people with responsibility

Here's a good way to build your organization and reputation, and at the same time minimize trouble in your department: give key people responsibility.

When I put a new head of a department, I instructed: "You're coming in here with a fresh perspective. I want you to challenge everything you see. I want you to get at the profit reason behind every action that's taken. If there's no profit purpose, eliminate the action. If you see something you don't like, change it. Or at least question it. Stick with the status quo and I'll assume that you subscribe to the action."

Then, I said that I'd be back from time to time to ask questions and I would want reasonable answers.

"I don't want assumptions," I said. "I want hardnosed explanations. In time, I'll expect you to be able to stand up like a trial attorney and defend everything that's being done in your department."

And I said one thing more: "The last person who held this job was unable to do this. That's why you have the job today."

Fourth: Convert subordinates into expert troubleshooters

Once, a credit supervisor came to me with an order in his hand, asking what to do with an account.

"We've been doing business with this company for almost five years. They owe us $10,000. Their account is four months past due. Now I've got a new order for $2,200," he stated. He filled in a few more facts: the customer's D&B rating, history, information about his operation. Then, he stopped talking and waited for an answer.

No answer. I sat there gazing at him. I didn't respond. The fellow shifted uneasily.

Finally, I said, "You're waiting. So am I. I'm waiting for the rest of the story; the second half."

He frowned, puzzled.

"What's your recommendation?" I fired at him. "You're the credit man. I want to know what you think we should do. If I don't agree with your judgment, I'll say so. If there's a problem you can't handle, I'll help you work it out if I can. But, I want your opinion. I want your thinking on the subject."

Get the point? My credit man did. It's a point I harp on regularly in our training and development program.

"Don't come to me with problems," I tell my people. "Come to me with ideas, actions, alternatives. Bring me answers."

Meet trouble head-on

The value is clear. When you force a person to tackle trouble, they develop the knack for coping with it. And, it helps them to overcome their fear of it. The more troubles you tackle, the less formidable they appear. My philosophy is: If you regard each trouble as a character-building and savvy-building experience, it will bring out the very best that is hidden within you. It goes for you. It goes for your people. It goes for all of us.

When the customer service department began receiving a rash of complaints, my troubleshooting flag popped 15 feet into the air. Step One: Track down the reason for the complaints. Customers were getting a lot of wrong merchandise.

I went down to the shipping department. "Bob, what's wrong? Why are so many shipments going out wrong?"

Bob frowned. "We're aware of the situation. We're studying it. Every time a complaint is called to our attention, we make a record of it."

"Fine," I pointed out. "At this rate, in three to six months, you'll have the answer. But that's not good enough. I want the answer now, today."

You know, in some companies, statistics are kept on everything. They're record-happy. They can trace back events and transactions to the Year One. You sometimes get the impression that the outfit is running a history class instead of a business.

"Bob," I said, "the record-keeping is fine. But in the meantime the customers are continuing to receive the wrong merchandise. Why?"

He had no answer, so we found one together. I picked up a shop order and looked at it. There were strange markings on the face of the document, instructions, directives. "Who puts on this stuff?" I asked. "Some of it looks pretty confusing to me."

"Well, it's copied in the factory from the original order," Bob replied.

"Who copies it? Let's go talk to him." We took a walk to see the man who did the copying. I pointed to the shop order I was holding in my hand. "Show me the original order from which this was developed."

The man dug into a file and pulled out the original order. There were two long paragraphs of instructions on the customer's document. The markings consisted of a condensation of these paragraphs. I could see at once that here was the root of the problem; it was written without the records, without the history.

"Let's call a meeting," I suggested. We kicked around the problem. We set up consistent standards and rules of procedure for transcribing instructions from original orders to shop orders. We made sure that each entry meant the same thing to each individual responsible for working with it. It was no longer left to the impressions and interpretations of one individual.

Action's what counts

What really counts in management is the action you take. One entrepreneur I knew put it this way, and I am in complete agreement: "To look is one thing. To see what you look at is another. To understand what you see is a third. To learn from what you understand is still something else. But to act on what you learn is all that really matters."

Fifth: Fire the right questions at the right people

When you begin troubleshooting, create your own personal questionnaire based on your experiences and observations recorded in your section or department or business. In working up your list, dig down deep. Get to the source of the action, the conflict, the document, or whatever.

Individualize your questions—keeping in mind the special characteristics, weaknesses, strengths and motivations of your people. First, pinpoint the problem. Then, pinpoint the questions that are most pertinent to the problem. And fire them at the people most directly responsible for the functions involved.

The more advanced your skill in this art, the more probing and sensitive your questions will become. The reward is clear. Uncover the right questions and the facts you want to know will come to light. For every question, there's an answer. For every answer, there's a process of logic and reasoning that takes place in the mind of the responder.

Sixth: To avoid or resolve troubles, keep the customer in mind

What do your company's customers mean to you? One manager answered the question as follows: "The customers don't need us; we need them. The customers are not an interruption of our work; they are the purpose of it. The customers are not an outsider to our business; they are the most vital part of it."

Nip trouble in the bud

More and more American companies today are going to considerable extremes to woo the customer and keep them won.

At the former Gates Rubber Co., for example, "the quality auditors" periodically visited key jobbers. The troubleshooting objective was to uncover product and operating deficiencies before customer irritation set in. The auditors tracked down product defects. They checked adherence to delivery schedules. They checked condition of merchandise on arrival, quality of service, paperwork errors, attention to adjustments and any other inconveniences possibly suffered by the customer.

I remember learning how Westinghouse Electric utilized another effective technique in its continuing effort to sidestep that familiar synonym for trouble—customer complaints—by having new product performance pretested in the homes of quality engineers. Their objective was clear: Pinpoint potential problems before they develop into the kind of trouble that spells disgruntled customers and reduced profits.

Seventh: Ward off trouble by putting yourself in the other guy's place

What makes a top-notch salesperson perform outstandingly? The ability to get into a prospect's mind and divine what they are thinking and how they will react. The first-rate troubleshooter operates the same way. They can climb into their customer's or somebody else's skin and access the product, the service, the operation, from their point of view.

Let me cite an example of one visit to a customer's place of business. Usually this man was happy to see me. This time, his greeting was a scowl. We had made a late shipment on an important job.

"May I see the bill of lading?" I asked.

All he had was a shipping notice. Without the bill, we were unable to actually pin down the date we shipped the order. But, the customer knew we were late. I promised to look into the situation immediately and returned to the plant.

Back at headquarters, I started making the rounds. I fired a battery of questions at different individuals. As I asked questions and explored the situation, I kept one person in the foreground of my mind at all times—that disgruntled customer. Each person I talked to had their own story, their own point of view, their own justification or rationalization for what had taken place.

I set up a new procedure so that the actual date of shipment was on the shipping notice, because the customer usually separates the bill of lading from the notice. Their accounting department must pay the shipping bill and match it with the bill of lading. Their order department keeps the shipping notice. Our system—putting shipment date on the bill of lading only—was fine for us but not good for the customer.

Put yourself in others' places

But, you can multiply this technique to encompass every individual with whom you deal. Master the art and you will add skill and power to your judgments and decisions. In tracking down trouble, or seeking to avert it, you'll be dealing with suppliers, competitors, associates, superiors, subordinates, and a host of other people.

You gave a subordinate an instruction. They didn't carry it out properly. Why not? Climb into their skin and find out. Was it due to some inherent weakness in their makeup? What could they gain by ignoring it or changing the procedure? There's a purpose behind every deed and every response. The place to search for the purpose is in the other person's mind.

A supplier promises delivery of a much-needed item. The item doesn't arrive. Why not? Shift your imagination and you may find out. Maybe they are overloaded with orders, short of people. They are aware your shipment is past due and vitally needed, but so are other shipments. Maybe your competitors are breathing down their neck harder than you are. Maybe their operation isn't big enough to cope with your needs. Maybe you're not big enough, from their point of view, to warrant priority over other more important customers. Where are the answers? In their mind.

You're a department head. One of your people starts making a rash of errors. Put yourself in their chair. Maybe the system has been changed and they have difficulty understanding the new way of doing things. Perhaps they are having family troubles and need a sympathetic ear. Observe. Probe. Analyze the operation and the individual who is operating. Latch on, if you can, to the other person's point of view.

The more advanced your skill in this art, the more probing and sensitive your questions will become.

As Henry Ward Beecher said: "Troubles are often the tools by which God fashions us for better things."

The trick is to face up to them and to train your people to do the same.

33

WRONG PHRASES THAT STOP A PROJECT

1. A good idea, but...
2. Against company policy
3. All right in theory
4. Be practical
5. Costs too much
6. Don't start anything yet
7. It needs more study
8. It's not budgeted
9. It's not good enough
10. It's not part of your job
11. Let's make a survey first
12. Let's sit on it for a while
13. That's not our problem
14. The boss won't go for it
15. The old timers won't use it
16. Too hard to administer
17. We have been doing it this way for a long time and it works
18. Why hasn't someone suggested it before if it's a good idea?
19. Ahead of the times
20. Let's discuss it
21. Let's go for a committee
22. We've never done it that way
23. Who else has tried it?

34

LEVINSONISMS

1. You are today a product of what you didn't do in the past.
2. Pay attention to the little things in your business life, and they will grow to be big things in your business.
3. Make developing people a major goal, and you will find that these people will be the major success story of your life.
4. Don't be mentally inefficient ... think total ideas ... don't be mentally absent.
5. Expand and sharpen your technique to visualize total ideas ... run your own mental television in your mind.
6. The only time you should use the word 'never,' is when you talk about the possibility of failure.
7. You get from people the example you set. Are you happy with your example?
8. Your enthusiasm must come from your inner perpetual motion machine ... it never stops.
9. Desire is the vehicle you ride to success.
10. If you're not having fun ... why take the trip?

ABOUT THE AUTHOR
ROBERT E. LEVINSON

After completing three years in the U.S. Navy, Levinson enrolled in Miami University (Ohio) where he received a Bachelor's degree in Business.

Following graduation, he joined his father and brother in their business, Steelcraft Manufacturing Company in Cincinnati, Ohio. The company was the largest manufacturer of steel doors and frames in the country. Over the years, he became primary executive of 14 additional family businesses.

In 1969, the company was sold to American Standard, Inc., where he became a Group Vice President in charge of 12 companies. During this time he developed, owned and operated three hotels in Broward and Palm Beach Counties, Florida.

In 1974, he received an honorary Doctor of Laws Degree from Miami University of Ohio.

After 10 years with American Standard, Levinson joined Lynn University in Boca Raton, Florida as Senior Development Officer.